Unofficial parkrun Guide
NEW ZEALAND

By Alison King

Front cover image by Andy Walmsley.

Book design by Alex Slack.

Printed in New Zealand

First printing edition 2021.

ISBN - 978-0-473-56996-9 (softcover)
ISBN - 978-0-473-56997-6 (softcover, print-on-demand)
ISBN - 978-0-473-56998-3 (Epub)
ISBN - 978-0-473-56999-0 (kindle)
ISBN - 978-0-473-57000-2 (pdf)

www.runswithabarcode.co.nz

Runs With A Barcode:

An unofficial guide to parkrun tourism in New Zealand

By Alison King

Join the Runs With a Barcode community at
FACEBOOK.COM/GROUPS/RUNSWITHABARCODECLUBHOUSE

Foreword

parkrun, spelt lowercase and always one word, is a bit pedantic these days.

You see all kinds of spellings and capitalisation these days and generally, I just take the view that the writer simply doesn't understand. But to many of the parkrun passionista, it hurts. Why, because no matter what your linguistic skills are, we accept that this is the moniker for something quite extraordinary.

It's the mark that highlights the way for a brilliant social experience. One where for most people there are no difficult situations, no complex issues or people that rub up against you.

No, indeed it's quite the opposite. parkrun offers a playground where you can get some exercise, exert some effort that you can control and do it in an easy, fun and enjoyable setting. Starting Bushy parkrun, Teddington, in the UK in October 2004 was my initial step towards providing a playground where friends could meet every Saturday to jog and chat over coffee.

It was so simple. You just arrived and ran.

When you finished you told me who you were and we all went for a coffee where I produced a set of results. What could be simpler?

What this grew into was unexpected. The world's largest series of running events taking place in just over 2000 locations each week.

Everyone is welcome from walker to Olympian and we all co-exist quite happily. There is something for everyone. It's a place and community where hearts and minds are calmed and even for some, healed.

Started in the UK and slowly expanding to Australia, South Africa, the USA and another 18, New Zealand came about because of my desire to involve my best friend and his wife, Noel and Lian de Charmoy in the movement. At the same time, a longstanding Kiwi friend Richard McChesney decided to transfer back home. It was a situation made in heaven.

Richard had participated and volunteered on many occasions and understood all the basics of what this movement stood for and it was then up to me to convince Noel and Lian to get involved. Lo and behold, here we are many years later with 30 events spread across New Zealand and over half a million finishers, parkrun New Zealand is well established.

I have visited a few New Zealand parkruns and seen a small part of the country and so I can testify to the magical nature of this land, the people and the movement that you have chosen to read about.

I am grateful for the many people like Alison who off their own back have decided to do something over and above to make parkrun even more special.

These people are a little army all of themselves. We call them the parkrun passionista. Some people refer to them as uber tourists and they are known for their focus and dedication to the cause.

I can never write about parkrun without thanking each and every person involved in its growth and operation. Our extraordinary movement is run mostly by volunteers and it is these people I feel I owe the most. They take on all the responsibilities involved in bringing you parkrun and in return they have their hearts filled with love and pride. An army built of passion, common understanding and the will to help others. Thank god for parkrun.

I hope you will enjoy Alison's book on New Zealand parkruns and the nature of the communities that thrive because of parkrun. I hope you are tempted to join us and discover the added joy that this brings.

Wishing you many happy adventures.

Paul Sinton-Hewitt
parkrun founder, Ashoka Fellow, FRSA

Introduction

My name is Alison King and I'm a parkrun addict.

It all started with a podcast and a wish to try this thing called parkrun. It resulted in a parkrun in my hometown, then came the quest to get the 50 milestone shirt, and an array of unofficial challenges then cropped up.

I can't say it's ended as I'm still parkrunning, though it's safe to say that it's taken over more of my life than I ever thought it would or could.

What parkrun has done for me is open my eyes to a new community of people who think nothing of getting up on a Saturday morning to go for a free 5km. It's also taken me to places I never would have considered before.

Regardless of where I am, whether in New Zealand or overseas, at my home parkrun or further afield, I know I will be among friends.

This book is designed to be a guide to touring as well as an historical document.

I've tried to speak to as many founding event directors as I can to get the background to their event. I've included information such as if there are showers nearby (so you can avoid staying parkrun fresh) and if the course is permanently marked. I've also included cancellation risk, which is typically low but there are some with planned cancellations.

Should you arrive at your destination the day before and realise you've forgotten your barcode I've also included how you can get a replacement printed.

There are also ideas on how to spend the rest of your weekend once you've got your parkrun fix (depending on how long you spend at the cafe!).

It's divided into North and South Island to help you plan a trip.

As parkrun is a moving feast with new events always in the planning stages I'd recommend you bookmark **www.runswithabarcode.co.nz** to subscribe find out about new events as they spring up.

Happy adventures!

Alison King - A2147564

All stats in this book were correct as of Jan 30 2021

History of parkrun in New Zealand

parkrun came to New Zealand by way of three people – country managers Noel and Lian de Charmoy and parkrunner Richard McChesney.

Noel and Lian de Charmoy

It was May 5th 2012 when parkrun officially took root in New Zealand, but the seeds were planted years earlier.

In fact, you could probably trace it right back to the 1980s, when parkrun founder Paul Sinton-Hewitt was working for Standard Bank in South Africa.

A few of the employees would run together at lunchtime.

"There were a couple of us who would do a lot of mileage," says Noel de Charmoy.

"There was myself, Brian Chamberlain (a South African marathon champion), a few others and Paul joined us. We all lived close together so we'd often run together. We just became family friends.

"There were lots of club runs on the weekends and during the week, usually around 8km, There was one around the corner from us that was 5km. We did it most Saturdays.

"It was a time trial and that's why Bushy Park was called a time trial when it originally started. It was really just for keen runners, no walkers at the back of the field like you find at parkrun now."

The de Charmoys go to Bushy

Paul moved to the UK in 1989 but the de Charmoys stayed in touch and visited him in London. They moved to New Zealand in 2002.

And then the Bushy Park Time Trial started in October 2004 with 13 runners.

"Paul came to visit us here in New Zealand in 2005 and told us about what is now parkrun," says Lian.

In 2009 they went to the UK and ran the Bushy Park event, now revered as the pilgrimage run. "We saw how it all worked and thought it was crazy. Even then Bushy had over 500 runners.

"Paul said parkrun was going to take off. After that the ball started rolling." He asked them on that visit if they would be parkrun country managers for New Zealand.

"We said it was a good idea but we were umming and ahhing about consents."

parkrun spreads

In 2011 parkrun launched in Australia (Main Beach parkrun, Queensland) and their home of South Africa (Delta parkrun, Johannesburg).

The de Charmoys were in Johannesburg early on in Delta's history – Delta Park is one of Noel's old training grounds. The country manager for South Africa is legendary runner – and another family friend – Bruce Fordyce so they found out more about how it all worked.

"When Richard McChesney approached Paul about starting Lower Hutt he came back to us about managing it all," says Noel.

"We said yes, let's go for it."

The pair met up with Richard at Auckland Airport as he made his way back to Wellington from the UK, describing him as "uber keen" to get parkrun started in his home country.

It was once Lower Hutt was off the ground that the de Charmoys realised they should have a parkrun in Auckland too. "And the rest is history," says Lian.

"It took another year to get Barry Curtis on the map but then it started rolling."

New Zealand's growth

The first few years the growth was slow, in 2012 there were just two events. In 2013 another three joined the fold (Barry Curtis, Porirua and Hamilton Lake). There were three more in 2014 (Dunedin, Millwater and Hagley) then two more in 2015 (Kapiti Coast and Western Springs).

In 2016 five events started up, taking parkrun New Zealand from 10 to 15 events between February and July that year. The following year was another slow burner with three events starting up but it was 2018 that led to an explosion in parkrunners. Noel says parkrun New Zealand set a parkrun record that year by growing by 50 per cent.

They started the year with 18 events and finished with 27. "All the growth is people who have run elsewhere and there wasn't a parkrun in their own town," says Noel. The couple get asked which is their favourite parkrun, an unfair question when each and every course has its highlights. "They're all great in their different ways, every event has something special," says Lian.

There have been events that have never eventuated for one reason or other – Kerikeri and Wellington Botanic Gardens among them.

The impact

"It's changed our lives in a way we never expected," says Lian.

"It's a happy place to be. Every new event that came along everyone was so keen and positive. We realise there's so many good people out there who are crazy about running/walking and wanting to embrace a healthy lifestyle. You meet people you only see on Saturdays and they become friends who you see on a weekly basis. We share stories, the good times and the bad times."

Noel agrees. "I do a lot of cycling and go out with a group of friends. The highlight is the chitchat but most importantly it's having a coffee afterwards. The vast majority of parkrun is about congregating with strangers – but really they're friends."

While they may no longer be country managers they are still involved with parkrun. Their daughter Caitlin is event director at Cornwall Park and you can often find them at the event. At the time of writing Lian was on 97 runs, although has far more volunteer roles (302).

"I loved my time with parkrun and Cornwall Park will always be our baby, but I'm loving the time with my twin grandsons and not having to do all the behind the scenes work," says Lian.

"I'm glad Paul asked us."

Richard McChesney – Event Director of Lower Hutt parkrun 2012-2014

"I've always said that if it wasn't me, someone else would have started the first parkrun in New Zealand, and eventually maybe in Lower Hutt, and maybe even on the same course. I just happened to be in the right place at the right time.

While I'm quite proud and see the growth I know that someone else would have done it. In 2008 I moved to the UK from New Zealand. I was a runner and I joined the local harrier club.

In my first or second week I was talking to someone about parkrun – Harrier runs were on Thursday, not Saturdays like back home.

I went home and registered. I turned up and was pretty much hooked from the start.

I did about 130 at 30 different venues through to 2011 and then we decided to move back to New Zealand with no idea of how long it would be for.

So I spoke to Paul Sinton-Hewitt and said I wanted to get it started in New Zealand. He told me country managers had been appointed in Noel and Lian but that they hadn't got around to doing anything yet.

When we decided to come back to New Zealand I did some deliberate parkrun tourism around the UK to get an idea of other courses to see how different courses operate.

I'd also not really gone to the cafe afterwards but I realised it was a community thing and that was one of the requirements in getting Lower Hutt set up."

The planning

"It had to be beside the Hutt River I thought, so I started looking at different options in the Hutt area.

Initially it was going to start on the other side of the river because there was a car park by the church and I arranged with the church to use the car park. But two or three weeks before we were due to start we had a whole lot of rain and there were too many puddles.

We would have gone up the trail on the opposite side of the river to Melling, then down the stopbank to the Ava railbridge, over the bridge and along the stopbank to finish where we now start and finish..

It's a slightly different course to what it is now. We changed it because it would have otherwise discouraged people in winter, so we decided to go out and back at the last minute.

The week before our first event we had more heavy rain. I did a trial run by myself and the new course seemed pretty good."

The inaugural event

"We got some publicity in the Hutt News and 86 runners turned up for our first event. I had no expectations but hoped it wouldn't be a complete flop.

Very quickly we developed a good community. People go to parkrun for the cafe and to meet their friends.

There are other people who go to do their veggie shop at the market afterwards. The run is something that's there. It's not necessarily the reason for being there.

The community is amazing, no one is a stranger. I've always had a rule that if I turn up alone and see someone else alone, I go and talk to them.

There are lots of amazing success stories as a result of parkrun.

There are others who don't necessarily have many friends or close family and parkrun is their family.

Our first Christmas Day people wouldn't have thought about it, but I'd been involved with Christmas Day parkruns in the UK. It's great for those people who would otherwise be alone that day and very popular."

North Island

Whangarei parkrun

Millwater parkrun

Hobsonville Point parkrun
Western Springs parkrun
Owairaka parkrun

Cornwall Park parkrun
Barry Curtis parkrun

Tauranga parkrun

Hamilton Lake parkrun
University of Waikato parkrun

Cambridge NZ parkrun

Puarenga parkrun

Gisborne parkrun

East End parkrun

Taupo parkrun

Anderson parkrun
Flaxmere parkrun

Whanganui Riverbank parkrun

Palmerston North parkrun

Kapiti Coast parkrun
Porirua parkrun
Trentham Memorial parkrun

Greytown Woodside Trail parkrun
Lower Hutt parkrun

Blenheim parkrun

Pegasus parkrun

Foster parkrun   Hagley parkrun

Wanaka parkrun

Queenstown parkrun

Dunedin parkrun

Invercargill parkrun   Balclutha parkrun

South
Island

North
Island

Photo Credit - Jan Sherley

Whangarei parkrun

131 Port Rd, Whangarei, 0110

Type of Course
Out and back in two directions.

Shoes Required
Road

Location of start
The run starts and finishes under Te Matau A Pohe bridge.

Getting there by public transport
There is no public transport available for this parkrun.

Getting there on foot
From the Town Basin follow the Hatea Loop past Reyburn House for about 1.5 km.

Getting there by road
Drive down Port Rd going past the Okara Centre by about 400m.Use the free car park on the left hand side next to Te Matau A Pohe Bridge.

Things to know

Toilets at the start/finish area, at the Pohe Island skateboard park and back at the Town Basin. Drinking water is available at the start/finish area and at several other locations on the course.

Parking is available in a large, free car park beside the start. Suitable for motorhomes.

Forgot your barcode? Email the RD to print for you.

Permanently marked.

Nearest showers at Whangarei Aquatic Centre.

Very low risk of cancellation.

AED at the start/finish.

Beware the bridge may open mid run.

Cafe

Christiez, by the start/finish area

Stats

First run: February 13, 2016

Inaugural attendance: 63

Record attendance: 211 (15/02/2020 and 22/02/2020)

Course Records

Women: Simone Ackermann 17:37 (17/10/2020)

Men: Luke Clements 15:55 (26/12/2020)

The Story Behind Whangarei parkrun...

Jim Kettlewell, founding event director

I was in Noosa, Queensland, looking for a running group to join while I was over there so I googled running in Noosa and up came this thing called parkrun.

I thought it sounded like a great idea and then found out it was all throughout Australia.

I never got to the Noosa event but I came back and was telling my friends at Hatea Harriers what I'd found. Someone said it was in New Zealand.

One guy was going down to North Auckland and doing it on a regular basis.

I looked up parkrun New Zealand and contacted them about starting up a parkrun in Whangarei.

Lian and Noel got back to me and said no one in Whangarei had yet contacted them and that if interested we could go ahead.

I'm president of Hatea Harriers and I talked to the club about parkrun and suggested we start one in Whangarei. It was seen as a good idea and from there we got going.

That was in September and we finally had our first run in February 2016.

As far as Hatea Harriers is concerned parkrun is one of the best things we've ever done as a club. It's brought a lot of people into running.

Athletics New Zealand asked me to speak at their conference about parkrun and how it has impacted us as a running club.

When we started we had no appreciation of what it was going to do. We've been getting 200 people on a regular basis. The new friendships we've made are amazing.

A lot of people tell us it's a highlight of their week. To hear that is such a buzz. I never envisaged that when we started.

Before we started council created the Hatea Loop in the basin, it's a 5km loop and it's become one of the most popular things the council has ever done, it was the obvious place for us to run.

But we've become a victim of our success and we're now looking at alternative courses because we can get overcrowded.

One feature we have is the bridge (Te Matau o Pohe) which opens for boats. It takes a few minutes and for visitors it's a highlight when it happens. It could be an issue if you're looking at a PB that day.

Whangarei Falls

 **While in Whangarei...**

Claphams National Clock Museum

Adventure Forest

Whangarei Art Museum

Mount Manaia

Whangarei Falls

Photo Credit - Kylie Crawford

Millwater parkrun

Sports fields, Millwater Parkway, Silverdale, Auckland 0932

Type of Course
Out and back.

Shoes Required
Road

Location of start
The start is a short walk from the Millwater Parkway Metro Park parking, adjacent to the bench located near to the public toilets.

Getting there by public transport
From the Hibiscus Coast Station and Park & Ride, take Bus 985. Stop at Bankside Road by Miller Rise (Stop ID: 4569).

Getting there on foot
From the bus stop on Bankside Road (Stop ID: 4569), head east on Bankside Road toward Founding Lane. Turn left onto Millwater Parkway.

Getting there by road

From the north: Take State Highway 1 exit 394 for Orewa. At the roundabout take the first exit for Grand Dr (Orewa). Turn right onto Arran Dr, go straight through one roundabout and then turn left at the next roundabout onto Millwater Parkway. Follow the road until you reach the sports fields on your right.

From the south: Take State Highway 1 exit 398 for Silverdale. At the roundabout take the third exit onto Hibiscus Coast Highway.

Turn left onto Silverdale St, and go over the first roundabout, continuing onto Silverdale St.

At the next roundabout take the first exit onto Millwater Parkway and follow the road until you see the sports fields on your right.

Parking is located on the right at Millwater Parkway Metro Park.

Things to know

Public toilets and parking in the Millwater Parkway Metro Park. Toilets are also approximately 1km along the course at the hockey fields.

Parking is free and there is space for motorhome parking.

Forgot your barcode? Email the RD to print for you

Permanently marked

Nearest showers at Northern Arena

Very low risk of cancellation – never cancelled

Cafe

Millie's Café, The Coffee Mill and Brotzeit German Bakery on Millwater Parkway all offer discounts on production of a parkrun barcode.

Stats

First run: September 20, 2014
Inaugural attendance: 56
Record attendance: 257 (25/01/2020)

Course Records

Women: Katrina Andrew 17:28 (07/12/2019)
Men: Mark Boyce 15:46 (28/11/2020)

The Story Behind Millwater parkrun...

Rhys Spyve, event director

There were two couples who started it off – the Myburghs and the Falconers. At the time Gavin Myburgh was involved with New Zealand Home Loans, the national sponsor of the time.

It was a very small parkrun to begin with. They'd get 20 and then 30 runners and then up to 60, all depending on the weather.

Then it grew steadily. I took over as event director in 2018 as Gavin and Antoinette were moving up north. I'd been run director and doing other volunteering.

I first heard of parkrun when I went to Australia in 2014 for a holiday to see my daughter. She asked me if I wanted to go and do a parkrun.

I asked her what it was and then said I wasn't sure if I could finish 5km. I thought it would take an hour.

Low and behold I went for a steady run and did it in 25:25. I was really happy with that. That was at Sandon Point. on the east coast of Sydney.

When I came home I looked up parkrun New Zealand to see what events there were and low and behold there was one in Millwater, only 20 minutes from where I was living at the time. I've since moved closer.

You see so many people turn up and they're all happy, motivated, the typical parkrun family stuff. There are so many people with a positive attitude.

You get to know a really good proportion of them. I don't know all 250 of them but we've a good core group of people involved. It starts the weekend off in a fantastic fashion. We get a few visitors, we've always got overseas runners and tourists from other parts of New Zealand.

We've got a thing called Millwater Magic, we've had so much luck when it comes to the weather. It can be raining cats and dogs on Friday and the forecast is rain for Saturday but there's no rain while we run and when we're done it starts to rain again.

It's become quite a thing that we get that good break in the weather.

I enjoy the run when I'm running, but it's the people who make it.

Wenderholm Regional Park

![camera icon] **While in north Auckland...**

Snowplanet

Silverdale Pioneer Village

Orewa Beach

Woodhill Mountain Bike Park

Wenderholm Regional Park walks

Photo Credit - Mike Beale

Hobsonville Point parkrun

Boundary Road, Hobsonville Point, Auckland, 0618

Type of Course
Out and back.

Shoes Required
Road

Location of start
The event starts about 300m past the wooden gate in the Meadow Clearing.

Getting there by public transport
Buses to Launch Rd: 112, 114. Use the Auckland Transport Journey Planner.

Getting there on foot
From bus stop on Launch Rd: Walk east along Launch Rd, at the bottom of the hill turn right at the roundabout.

To the right of the roundabout is a road that can only be accessed on foot via the side of the gate. Follow the road about 300m.

Getting there by road

From the North Shore head southeast on State Highway 18. Exit onto Squadron Dr.

Turn left onto Hobsonville Point Rd, which leads into Hudson Bay Rd. Turn right onto Launch Rd and park on either side.

From central head northwest on State Highway 16. Keep left at the fork to continue onto State Highway 18 andfollow signs for North Shore/Hobsonville Rd/32.

Take exit 19A for Hobsonville Rd, keep left to continue toward Hobsonville Rd.

Turn right onto Hobsonville Rd and keep right to stay on Hobsonville Rd.

Continue onto Hobsonville Point Rd, which leads into Hudson Bay Rd. Turn right onto Launch Rd and park on either side.

Parking can be found along both sides of Launch Rd, to the left of Boundary Rd (the wharf side), the corner of Launch Rd and Bomb Point Dr and along the northern end of Bomb Point Dr.

Once parked head to the bottom of Launch Rd. At the bottom of the hill turn right at the roundabout where you will find a road that can only be accessed on foot via the side of the gate. The start is at the base of the wooden stairs that lead up the hill.

Things to know

Toilets located down at the wharf and also at the Music Hub off Catalina Bay Dr. There is ample free parking along Launch Rd.

Te Onekiritea Point (Bomb Point) was once the site of New Zealand's largest Air Force explosives depot.

Forgotten your barcode? Email the RD to see if they can print off for you. Otherwise visit Warehouse Stationery at Albany Mega Centre (7A/140 Don McKinnon Dr).

Not permanently marked

No showers nearby

Low risk of cancellation

Pacers on the second Saturday of the month

Cafe
Fabric Café Bistro, located directly opposite the wharf.

Stats

First run: May 18, 2019

Inaugural attendance: 239

Record attendance: 311 (01/01/2020)

Course Records

Women: Hannah Oldroyd 18:07 (01/02/2020)

Men: Greg Darbyshire 16:04 (18/05/2019)

The story behind Hobsonville Point parkrun...

Scott Arrol, run director

"Event director Shontelle Clarke had been quietly working away on it for quite some time before it got started. It goes back to when Noel and Lian were still country managers, it was probably the last parkrun that they helped get going.

Shontelle was a walker at Western Springs parkrun, she fell in love with parkrun and wanted to have one out at Hobsonville Point where she lives.

Gary Kelly and I were running together and we'd been talking about getting parkrun going in Albany, then someone mentioned Shontelle. The next time we were there we introduced ourselves. She'd got to the point where she needed more support.

There were a couple of courses mapped out. Gary and I ran those and said which we preferred. Then a few more people came on board to help get it started.

It's not on council land. It was government-owned land but then the land was vested into a company and that's how the development was started. We had to get their permission and that was more time-consuming than a problem.

It took off right from the outset. The parkrun growth is from young families and other young people living out there. We had big numbers for the first event and it kept on growing.

Shontelle was the driver of it but I'm sure there would have been parkrun there eventually. She was just so determined."

 While in Hobsonville Point...

Visit the Hobsonville Point Farmers Market in its historic seaplane hangar.

Visit Muriwai's gannet colony, best seen between August and March.

Got kids? Spend some time at the award-winning Hobsonville Point playground, drive down Buckley Ave.

You'll have run through it for parkrun but explore Te Onekiritea Point (Bomb Point), once the site of New Zealand's largest Air Force explosives depot. Walk or cycle the track around the perimeter and look out for the 12 Defence Force munitions bunkers dating back to the Second World War that still dot the landscape today.

Walk the Didsbury Art Trail.

Muriwai's gannet colony

Photo Credit - John Heron

Western Springs parkrun

Western Springs Park, Motions Rd, Auckland 1022

Type of Course
Three Laps

Shoes Required
Road

Location of start
The run starts at the entrance to Western Springs Park from the Auckland Zoo car park.

Getting there by public transport
Buses can be caught to Auckland Zoo from across Auckland. See the Auckland Transport website for more information. From Britomart, bus numbers 30, 80, 90, 115, 135, 153 and 195 can all be used. Alight at stop number 8124.

Getting there on foot
Stop 8124 is at the corner of Great North and Motions Rd. Walk down Motions Rd until you reach the entrance to Auckland Zoo. If you turn right into the entrance way, the

Western Springs parkrun starts at the beginning of Western Springs Park, up the small rise in front of you.

Getting there by road
Drive from the city on State Highway 16 towards Helensville, take exit 6 for Saint Lukes Rd. Turn right onto St Lukes Rd (signs for Port Chevalier/Western Springs). Turn left onto Great North Rd. Turn right onto Motions Rd. Turn right at the entrance to the Auckland Zoo. Parking is available in the Zoo's car park.

Things to know
Plenty of free parking available in the Auckland Zoo car park. Public toilets and a children's playground are available near the course start. The zoo opens at 9.30am.

Forgotten your barcode? Print out at Grey Lynn or Pt Chevalier libraries or Warehouse Stationery, St Lukes.

Permanently marked

There are no showers nearby

Very low risk of cancellation (annual cancellation for Pasifika Festival in March)

Pacing event last Saturday of the month

Cafe
Weta Café, Auckland Zoo, opens at 8.30am.

Stats

First run: November 21, 2015

Inaugural attendance: 95

Record attendance: 246 (11/01/2020)

Course Records

Women: Rebekah Greene 17:42 (03/11/2018)

Men: Oliver Mott 15:53 (05/01/2019)

The Story behind Western Springs parkrun...

Michael Jenkinson, event director

Mike Wilkinson, the original ED asked me to be involved right from the start. I didn't know about parkrun, we were in the same running club, TempoFit. A lot of us did the parkrun course the week before it started, as a trial run.

I couldn't do the first one – our anniversary falls on the same day as other events. It was quite social from the start, there were a lot of runners from our running club. I was able to meet up with like-minded people, have a run and then a coffee.

Mike asked me to help a bit more, I didn't know him until a few months before parkrun started. When we started we had a lot of beginner runners who did the Couch to 5km programme. They'd come along and improve every week. They started by walking and now some are sub 25. We see the change in people and that's what I enjoy. We get quite a few visitors because we're close to the city. As you start, on the left are the elephants and often they're standing watching parkrunners. You can walk right up to the back fence and see the elephant enclosure. We often hear the lions roaring as we set up. * The elephants are leaving Auckland Zoo 2021.

While in Auckland...

Auckland Zoo

MOTAT

Skytower

Auckland Museum

Visit Waiheke Island

Waiheke Island.

Owairaka parkrun

Owairaka Park, 56-60 Owairaka Avenue, Mt Albert, 1025 Auckland

Type of Course
Out and back in two directions

Shoes Required
Road

Location of start
The start is at the bottom of Owairaka Park, near the end of Hendon Ave.

Getting there by public transport
The 24R bus goes from Victoria St in the CBD to Owairaka Ave. Get off the bus at Stop number 8810, right outside the park.

Bus route 66 travels east/west from Pt Chev to Sylvia Park (and vice versa). Get off at Stop 8820 or 8829 on Mt Albert Rd, and walk to the park via Owairaka Ave (10 minutes). Similarly, bus route 670 travels between New Lynn and Otahuhu and stops on Stoddard Rd, Stop 8270, and walk (15 minutes) via Richardson Rd and Owairaka Ave.

The nearest train station is Mt Albert, on the Western Line. Owairaka Park is 2.1km from the train station by foot (warmup distance), via New North Rd, turning left onto Richardson Rd, then left onto Owairaka Ave. Alternatively, the 66 bus is a short walk from the station (see the previous page).

Getting there on foot
The main entrance to Owairaka is at 56-60 Owairaka Ave. Follow the path to the start/finish area at the bottom of the park. This is adjacent to the road end at 209 Hendon Ave.

Other points of access close by lead to the bike path across the bridge from the start/finish area, including Wainwright Ave, O'Donnell Ave, Richardson Rd, McGehan Close and Beagle Ave.

Getting there by road
Coming via the motorway from the northwest, north and CBD, come through the Waterview Tunnel on SH20 and take the first exit, Number 19, at Maioro Rd. Turn left onto Maioro Rd, left onto Stoddard Rd, then merge right onto Richardson Rd. Turn right onto Hendon Ave at the next traffic lights and continue to the end of Hendon Ave (or continue to the main park entrance via Hallam St and Owairaka Ave).

Coming via the motorway on SH20 from the southeast, exit at Maioro Rd, Exit 19, then turn right onto Maioro St, then continue as above.

From surrounding suburbs, Owairaka Ave can be accessed from Richardson Rd to the south or Mt Albert Rd in the north.

Things to know

Owairaka Park has a children's play area including a flying fox, skatepark and basketball half-courts. There are public toilets by the carpark, which has 35 spaces. Near the parkrun start/finish area is a community garden. Adjacent to the bike path on the course are a BMX pump track and Māra Hūpara, a traditional Maori play area, both only a two minute walk away.

There is additional road parking on Owairaka Ave, Hendon Ave (northern end), Wainwright Ave (off O'Donnell Ave) and other surrounding streets. Motorhomes will have to park on the street.

Forgotten your barcode? Head to Mount Albert Library, open until 6pm on Fridays.

The course is not permanently marked.

Nearest showers at Mount Albert Aquatic Centre on Alberton Ave.

Low risk of cancellation

Cafe
L'Oeuf, 4a Owairaka Ave

Stats

First run: October 24 2020

Inaugural attendance: 209

Record attendance: 209 (24/10/2020)

Course Records

Women: Hannah Oldroyd, 19:31 (31/10/2020)

Men: Paul Martelletti, 14:58 (16/01/2021)

The store behind Owairaka parkrun...

Julie Collard, event director

It's been a long time coming. I'm relatively new to parkrun but I heard about it a long time ago. I'm a teacher and I've had a run club going since 2014. A girl who was a very good runner at the school told me about this thing called parkrun. I thought it was a silly name. She said it was free and I was kind of suspicious.

I've always been a runner and I've been involved with our running club since my daughter was 5. I had belonged to an athletics club when I was a kid.

It was quite a famous club, Owairaka Athletics Club. It has a long history. Olympians Peter Snell and Murray Halberg were from this club and their coach Arthur Lydiard too. It so happened that the president was getting the club restarted, it was really small so I became a committee member and got involved with coaching.

So I was suspicious of this free thing because not much comes for free. Then over the years I heard it was for real. With my family we were getting more involved with running so in January 2017 we went along to Cornwall parkrun and we loved it from day one.

The second week we went to Western Springs and loved that even more so I switched my home run and we've been there ever since. After my third or fourth time I volunteered and loved that as well. It was a natural fit.

Right from the beginning I had this idea for Owairaka parkrun. I love choosing different routes and going to new places to explore. My family always complains that I'm always thinking about parkrun courses.

I mentioned about starting a new one up to Pete Kenny, a run director at Western Springs – and committee member at OAC. He said I needed to be a run director, so I did that for two years.

I had lots of ideas but the one place I was fixed on was near my home, but it has a car park in the middle of it. Suddenly this route became available. It was close to my athletics club and we used it for training a lot, but it was closed for ages because the council were re-doing the path and doing amazing work with the stream.

They've built a bridge connecting the creek with the park. All these years there's been nothing connecting them other than a pipe. They also put in an underpass under Richardson Rd and that's opened up the possibility of a longer run without crossing roads.

It opened over a year ago and the club held a fun run. The start/finish area is across the stream from the former house of Arthur Lydiard. There's a lot of history there. It's a really cool location.

I contacted Noel and Lian and they were very enthusiastic but it was just before they stepped down as country managers and parkrun NZ became under the Asia Pacific umbrella.

We got lost for a while but then Kent Stead became an ambassador. I know him from Western Springs parkrun, so we got going. He brought his family over and we measured the course together with his wheel. I'm a teacher and it was school holidays so I got on with the paperwork.

There were times when I thought it was going to fall apart due to the funding aspect. Then we found out all we needed to do was fund a defibrillator. Then Covid hit and everything shut down.

My club was going to buy a defib and we were going to share it but then parkrun said that wouldn't work, but not to worry as there was an organisation that funds a certain amount of defibs each year. That solved that problem. There's been so much encouragement. At Western Springs people have known about it for a while and are always asking about it.

After the defib was sorted I had a bit of paperwork to do and we were approved by parkrun global in early September.

Ambury Regional Park

📷 **While in Auckland...**

Visit heritage property Alberton House

Take a walk by Oakley Creek, the longest stream in the Auckland isthmus

Mount Albert Aquatic Centre wave pool

There are several heritage walks around Mount Albert

Visit Ambury Regional Park

Photo Credit - Dylan Logan

Cornwall Park parkrun

Cornwall Park, Greenlane West, Auckland

Type of Course
Three laps mixed terrain

Shoes Required
Road or trail

Location of start
The event starts at the Band Rotunda (near the café).

Getting there by public transport
Please check Auckland Transport's Journey Planner.

Stop 7612 at Great South Rd/Greenlane, Opp 205 Great South Rd, is the closest to the Main Gates of Cornwall Park and is a 20 minute walk to parkrun.

The 70 service from Symonds St leaves for this stop every 15 minutes.

Getting there on foot
There are three entrances from Campbell Rd, one at the top of Onehunga Mall going in at Grand Drive and another near Rawhiti Rd entering in at Bollard Ave. There is no vehicle access here.

There is also a footpath entrance opposite Horotutu Rd. There is another footpath entrance at the junction of Maungakiekie Ave (off Greenlane Rd) and Atarangi Rd, which is the closest entrance to the Band Rotunda.

Getting there by road
Main entrance is on Greenlane West Rd, at the traffic lights with Puriri Rd (which is very close proximity to the ASB Showgrounds). Turn into Cornwall Park onto Pohutukawa Dr.

From Manukau Rd there are two entrances, one near the Stardome Observatory in One Tree Hill and the other at Campbell Cres which leads into Puriri Rd and straight on to the Main Gate of Cornwall Park. Greenlane Rd is also accessible from the motorway, exit 433.

Things to know
Toilets are in the Pohutukawa Dr car park. There is ample free parking. There is space for motorhome parking.

Forgotten your barcode? Email the RD to see if they can print off for you.

The course is not permanently marked.

There are no showers nearby.

Low risk of cancellation

There is minimal signage in this park, head to the band rotunda for parkrun.

Cafe
Cornwall Park Café, beside the finish.

Stats

First run: July 28, 2012

Inaugural attendance: 35

Record attendance: 420 (01/02/2020)

Course Records

Women: Becky Wade 17:44 (02/03/2013)

Men: Jonathan Jackson 15:49 (10/12/2016)

The store behind Cornwall Park parkrun...

Caitlin Barton, event director

I've been involved right from the start because mum and dad were country managers (Noel and Lian de Charmoy stepped down in November 2019).

Cornwall Park wasn't the first to start but it was the one my parents got going.

We opened a couple of months after Lower Hutt, we would have opened before them but because we're in a private park we had to make the park trust comfortable with what we were going to do.

They'd never had an event like this before and they're very strict about numbers.

At our first run we had 35 runners, which isn't a lot but

enough to be scary – that 35 people had heard about it and they weren't all family or friends. There were people we didn't know.

Because my parents are friends with [parkrun founder] Paul Sinton-Hewitt it's one parkrun where he organised the course before it went live.

They went to Cornwall Park multiple times, because parkrun has criteria for courses it was interesting to do it with the head honcho.

We didn't really have to think about it because he was directing the course in a very natural manner.

Since then it's been changed.

We've grown from strength from strength. We always knew numbers would grow to a decent size but it's happened in parkrun's traditional sense, slow growth over the years.

That's how Paul told us to do it throughout the whole of New Zealand.

The café wasn't there when we started. We used to go to one down the road but after a while there were people standing outside as it had got so busy.

The park built a new café but it is right where we used to start the run. We turned up one Saturday to find the start line was a building site. It was three weeks out from opening when it burned to the ground. We arrived as the fire brigade were putting it out.

Cornwall Park is a beautiful private park, unique in Auckland. We run in such a small part of it. There's One Tree Hill where you can get a view of all of Auckland, multiple cafes and so many different elements to the park.

When we started Cornwall parkrun we had an expectation of how it would grow because of knowing Paul and seeing how it had grown in the UK and South Africa.

Being a part of it has been much more amazing than what we thought it could be in the beginning.

I love the community that's evolved over the years.

 While in Auckland...

Explore Cornwall Park

Stardome Observatory Planetarium

Parnell Rose Gardens

La Cigale French Market

Kelly Tarlton's Sealife Centre

Photo Credit · Carin Newbould

Barry Curtis parkrun

Barry Curtis Park, Stancombe Road, Flat Bush, Auckland, 2016

Type of Course
Two laps

Shoes Required
Road

Location of start
The run starts opposite the Wetland playground off Stancombe Rd.

Getting there by public transport
A number of bus stops traveling in all directions can be found on Stancombe Rd and Chapel Rd. Use the Auckland Transport Journey Planner to plan your journey.

Getting there on foot
Barry Curtis Park is a large park in the middle of the Flat Bush suburb. It is easily accessible by foot from a number of points.

Getting there by road

From the north: Follow State Highway 1 south to exit 444, East Tamaki Rd/Urban Route 8. Turn left. Turn right onto Preston Rd then left onto Ormiston Rd. Turn left onto Chapel Rd then right onto Stancombe Rd.

From the south: Follow State Highway 1 north to exit 449A-B towards Manukau. Turn right at the Great South Rd lights and then keep in the right lane at the next lights to run right onto Redoubt Rd. Turn left onto Hollyford Drive, right onto Aspiring Ave, continue straight onto Matthews Ave, which leads to Chapel RD, then right onto Stancombe Rd.

Things to know

Toilets, a children's playground and water (drinking) fountains are available. There is ample free parking in the car park accessed opposite Erica Rd.

Parking is free and there is space for motorhome parking.

Permanently marked

Forgotten your barcode? Botany Libray at Botany Town Centre is open until 8pm on a Friday.

No showers nearby

Very low risk of cancellation

Barry Curtis Park is the largest urban park to be developed in Auckland in the last 100 years.

Cafe

Sequel Café, 16J Bishop Dunn Pl.

Stats

First run: May 25, 2013

Inaugural attendance: 36

Record attendance: 261 (01/02/2020)

Course Records

Women: Lisa Cross 18:00 (13/04/19)

Men: Peter Wheeler 15:15 (30/06/2018)

The story behind Barry Curtis parkrun...

Tom Mann, founding event director

I was doing a bit of work with the Auckland Council at the time and was in the event space getting people active. We'd been throwing the idea around about starting a run group.

When you type in the words park and run to Google, parkrun comes up. Chris Earl, who was with the parks department, went and did a few runs at Cornwall parkrun and got a feel for what parkrun is.

We talked with Noel and Lian and the messaging around it being a volunteer organisation for the community. We thought it was something we needed to think about as we were paid employees. We thought we'd have to do it with a different hat but we wanted to keep the council in the picture.

My girlfriend at the time, Esther (now my wife), myself and Chris, after working with Noel and Lian, decided that Barry Curtis Park would be a good fit for parkrun – we'd first looked at Totara Park.

We were a bit sceptical at first because it was a new park with not many established trees. I didn't think a two lap course would be very fun but it is really a cool thing. It was relatively easy to map it out because there are a lot of paths that cut through the park. It took around two to three months of working with Noel and Lian, who were amazing.

It's been fascinating watching the growth on a national and international scale. We had low numbers for a number of years and then it started to grow. It's totally gone beyond what we imagined.

It's everything what a council wants – a volunteer driven programme to deliver a positive social and physical project for the community. Councils should be throwing hundreds of thousands of dollars at parkruns across the country because of the positives it's doing for communities.

The best thing about Barry Curtis is watching the people who run PBs, not the sub 20s but the plus 35s, those who have turned up and they keep coming back as it's made such a change in their lives.

It's a pretty special feeling seeing these people doing things and make these positive changes. There's also the sense of community, as a result of parkrun there's now a Sunday cycling group, they run on Saturday then bike together Sunday. One thing I love about Barry Curtis is we're never the biggest, being small we've kept that strong community feel to it.

The park is named after a former mayor of the then Manukau City Council, and we run along the John Walker Promenade, which is cool that we're keeping his legacy going.

Fo Guang Shan Buddhist Temple

📷 **While in South Auckland...**

Auckland Botanic Gardens

Howick Historical Village

Fo Guang Shan Buddhist Temple

Rainbow's End

Clevedon Farmer's Market on Sundays

Hamilton Lake parkrun

Hamilton Lake, Innes Common, Hamilton 3204

Type of Course
One big lap and one small lap

Shoes Required
Road

Location of start
The event starts on the grass beside the car park entrance.

Getting there by public transport
From the Hamilton Transport Centre take bus 29 for the 10 minutes trip to Hamilton Lake. From the drop off point it is a 800m walk around the lake edge to the race start.

For the bus route and current timetable please check the busit website.

Getting there on foot
At the Hamilton Yacht Club off Lake Domain Dr, Hamilton on the Innes Common side of the Hamilton Lake.

Getting there by road

From the north, follow State Highway 1 into Hamilton. Turn left onto Killarney Rd. Turn right onto Lake Domain Dr and follow until the Hamilton Yacht Club car park is on your left.

From the south, follow State Highway 1 to the intersection with State Highway 3 (Ohaupo Rd). Turn right. Turn left onto Lake Cres and drive until you see the Hamilton Yacht Club car park on your right.

Things to know

There are toilets and a children's playground beside the start. Free parking is available in the Hamilton Yacht Club car park and on Lake Domain Dr. Motorhome friendly.

Permanently marked

Forgotten your barcode? Email the RD to see if they can print off for you.

No showers nearby

Low risk of cancellation

Cafe

Cafe Fresca, 78 Alison St, Hamilton Lake.

Stats

First run: October 19, 2013

Inaugural attendance: 59

Record attendance: 305 (12/09/2015)

Course Records

Women: Lesley Van Miert 16:58 (8/2/2014)

Men: Jacob Priddey 15:02 (31/08/2019)

The Story Behind Hamilton Lake parkrun...

Rob Hammington, founding event director

I was President of Hamilton Road Runners. One of our club members came to me one day saying a friend of his was the local franchisee of New Zealand Home Loans (first sponsor of parkrun New Zealand). He wanted to set up a parkrun here in Hamilton and could I help.

I said "parkwhat?" I had no idea what it was, this was way back in early 2013 approximately. It then transpired the person he was talking about was someone I used to work for – Dave Hale. So I went to see him, he told me what parkrun was about and said "I don't know a thing about running but can you help us?" I said "hell yeah".

It was difficult, because parkrun starts at 8am and Hamilton Road Runners have a Saturday morning session at the same place.

The concern then was that it would ruin the club but it's saved it, because it recruits without trying. The club is now made up largely of parkrunners. We had 59 at our first event, I'm very, very proud of what's been achieved at Hamilton Lake.

To me it's a typical parkrun, it's the people who make the parkrun.

I could see the potential for it. It's better than I ever thought it would be. I liked what it does for the community and for a lot of individuals. Physical health, mental health. I've known quite a few people who go to parkrun for their mental wellbeing and they create great friendships.

Quite a few of our parkrunners have gone on to run in ultras, it's been a good stepping stone.

I'll be parkrunning until I drop. I'm addicted to it, it's like a drug. It's part of my life now. I love the people. We've had some notable runners. One day back in 2014 I was setting up and this tall runner showed up. We had no idea who she was. She asked where the run went and when we started she went off so fast. Turned out she was a European running champion. We were so thrilled to have her here (Lesley Van Miert's course record of 16:58 still stands at the time of writing).

We've had Dave Moorcroft – the former 5000m world record holder – too. That was something special, he was here for my last stint as run director (in February 2020).

I don't travel the world to do a parkrun but if I'm where there is a parkrun I will do it.

Hamilton Gardens.

While in Hamilton...

Hamilton Gardens

Hamilton Zoo

Waikato River Explorer

Bridal Veils Falls

Zealong Tea Estate

Photo Credit - Alison King

University of Waikato parkrun

University of Waikato, Gate One, Knighton Road, Hamilton East, Hamilton 3240

Type of Course
Multi loop course with a mix of scenery

Shoes Required
Road

Location of start
The Village Green

Getting there by public transport
The Clockwise Orbiter bus arrives on Knighton Rd right by the University of Waikato. You can enter through Gate 2A and follow the path past Unirec to the village shops. There will be signage out, so follow the signs. Go to www.busit.co.nz for timetable information.

Getting there on foot
Enter the University of Waikato campus at Gate Two off Knighton Rd, follow the path past UniRec towards the shops. Just before the shops turn left to the Village Green, the meeting point is under the shops shelter.

Getting there by road
Turn off Knighton Rd into Gate One and enter the car park on the left. The start at the Village Green is approximately 150m from the car park

There is no charge for parking on campus on the weekend.

Things to know
There is ample free parking at the university with space for motorhomes. The 5km course runs around the beautiful park-like grounds and lakes of the University of Waikato. The course includes artworks and botanical planting of interest, it passes the Gallagher Academy of Performing Arts and a fitness island and provides attractive campus vistas.

Free parking is located in Gate One, Knighton Rd.

Toilets are available within the Village Green shops

Forgot your barcode? Email unirec@waikato.ac.nz before 3pm on the Friday prior to the event. You will need to collect the printed barcode from UniRec reception. They open at 7am on Saturday mornings.

Permanently marked

Nearest showers at UniRec, towel hire available

Low risk of cancellation

Cafe
Jacks Coffee Lounge, 1/31 Cambridge Rd.

Stats
First run: November 7 2020
Inaugural attendance: 190
Record attendance: 190 (7/11/2020)

Course Records

Women: Frances Stringfellow, 19:59 (7/11/2020)

Men: Dean Chiplin, 17:32 (19/12/2020)

The Story Behind University of Waikato parkrun...

Nicola Clayden, founding event director

I'm the sport development manager at the university. I'd put the parkrun happening down to a project called Living Campus Project to make the campus a more user-friendly space for the community.

Lots of ideas were thrown around. It's a beautiful campus with walking tracks, feature gardens and art. There was an idea of making a designated distance track for running and walking. We've got Lex Chalmers on campus, he's been involved with Hamilton Road Runners and Hamilton Lake parkrun. If it wasn't for him this wouldn't be happening.

He helped come up with this; parkrun was mooted but he's been the one who has driven it in terms of the course. He's measured it out many, many times. We've been working on this for about 12 months, with Covid thrown in as well it's been quite a long process.

Lex is the passion and I'm the doer, together we've made it happen. My role involves looking at ways to get students and staff active, parkrun ticks all the boxes.

The University of Waikato also encourages students to get involved in volunteering, through Work Integrated Learning and the Employability Plus Programme. Setting up parkrun presents a great opportunity to volunteer, to give back to the local community, gain some experience for their CV and be acknowledged.

We hope we get some really passionate people involved and will thrive in that community. For student involvement it's great. We know that students who get involved in something other than their studies gain positive benefits on their wellbeing and development.

The fact it's a global organisation and there's a community beyond Hamilton is really cool.

While at the University of Waikato...

After parkrun you can explore the 65 hectare University of Waikato campus.

There are three small community gardens on campus, as well as a Rongoā Māori medicinal garden, a threatened plant garden, over 6,000 mature trees and a diverse native bird life, including tui and a resident ruru. The University also has a vast native fern collection hosting more than 70 New Zealand ferns, including three mature Kahikatea stands.

Check out the Gallagher Academy of Performing Arts for any weekend performances.

Local Bites Food Market is on campus every Saturday from 4pm.

About University of Waikato

As one of New Zealand's leading institutions for teaching and research, the University of Waikato has 12,500 students and 1600 staff across two vibrant campuses in Hamilton and Tauranga,

The University's diverse and welcoming student community includes a strong Māori and Pacific Island presence (29% of the domestic student population), along with 2,500 international students from more than 70 countries.

The University has a further 670 students at its joint institute with Zhejiang University City College (ZUCC) in China.

Students at Waikato enjoy quality learning experiences and smaller class sizes, flexible degree structures, work-integrated learning to ensure they are industry ready, and supportive research supervision from internationally acclaimed academics. The University also delivers world-leading research, particularly in the areas of environmental sustainability, cyber security and safety, physical and mental health, and indigenous wellbeing.

Photo Credit - Alison King

Cambridge NZ parkrun

Avantidrome, 15 Hanlin Rd, Cambridge 3283

Type of Course
Out and back

Shoes Required
Road

Location of start
The event starts near the Avantidrome car park.

Getting there by public transport
The 20 service leaves from the Cambridge i-Site and stops at the Avantidrome. See the Busit website for timetable.

Getting there on foot
From Cambridge township Head northwest on Thermal Explorer Hwy/Victoria St turn left into Hamilton Rd which becomes Cambridge Rd turn left onto St Peters School Rd, destination on left.

Getting there by road
From Cambridge township head northwest on Thermal Explorer Hwy/Victoria St turn left into Hamilton Rd which becomes Cambridge Rd turn left onto St Peters School Rd, destination on left.

From Hamilton follow State Highway 1 south. Take the Cambridge West exit, turn right into St Peters School and left onto St Peters School Rd then right onto Hanlin Rd and park at the Avantidrome.

Things to know
There is ample free parking at the Avantidrome and toilets in the car park. Parking suitable for motorhomes.

Forgot your barcode? Email the RD to print out.

Not permanently marked

No showers nearby

Very low risk of cancellation

Cafe
The Bikery Café & Catering (at Avantidrome).

Stats

First run: March 4, 2017

Inaugural attendance: 95

Record attendance: 170 (01/01/2019)

Course Records

Women: Charli Miller 18:57 (03/03/2018)

Men: Jonny McKee 16:28 (25/01/2020)

The Story Behind Cambridge NZ parkrun...

Brian Prescott, event director

I hadn't even been to a parkrun when Rob Hammington and Lex Chalmers from Hamilton Lake were looking at setting up Cambridge parkrun.

They had put a few words out around the place. Someone mentioned me and then somehow I ended up as event director.

Rob and Lex set it up and I took it over and I'm still here. It took me six months before I got to run one. I've run 69 now.

We've quite a good rivalry with Cambridge parkrun in the UK. We've had a few visitors from Cambridge UK.

It took a year before anyone had run the double but there are quite a few now, but we've not had anyone go over there to run their one.

We were set up as an overspill to Hamilton Lake, they were well-established and thinking it could expand. Originally they looked at starting at the Gaslight Theatre end, which is where we turn around but there's no toilets or cafe.

The Avantidrome gives us those facilities and some character. We've a brutal short hill at the end but it's all psychological.

There aren't many parkruns to have their name and country in the title, there are quite a few twins in Australia (same name as a parkrun or town in the UK), but we're the only one in New Zealand.

While in Cambridge...

Avantidrome

Lake Karapiro

Sanctuary Mountain/Maungatautiri

Waikato River Trails

Hobbiton Tour

Photo Credit - Alison King

Tauranga parkrun

Kopurererua Valley Reserve, Tauranga, 3110

Type of Course
Out and back

Shoes Required
Road

Location of start
The event starts by the skate park on 17th Ave West.

Getting there by public transport
To catch a bus to Tauranga parkrun refer to the Bay Bus schedule.

Getting there on foot
Tauranga parkrun can be accessed from various access points on the boardwalk or from walking down 17h Ave West from Cameron Rd.

Getting there by road
From the northern or southern ends of the city travel along Cameron Rd until you reach the 17th Ave traffic lights. You then drive down the hill (on your right from the city end and left from the Greerton end) and park at the end of 17th Ave West where you will see the Māori pou marking the start point by the skate park.

Things to know
Public toilets in The Historic Village and ample free parking on 17th Ave West. The Historic Village has an array of shops. Parking suitable for motorhomes.

Permanently marked

Forgot your barcode? Email the RD to print for you or print at Warehouse Stationery on Friday.

Nearest showers at Greerton Pool

Very low risk of cancellation

Can arrange pick up from cruise ships

Cafe
The Whipped Baker, in the Historic Village, 17th Ave West

Stats
First run: April 28, 2018
Inaugural attendance: 272
Record attendance: 272 (28/04/2018)

Course Records
Women: Hannah Wells 17:29 (26/01/2019)
Men: Hayden Wilde 14:57 (18/01/2020)

The Story Behind Tauranga parkrun...

Peter East, co-event director

I started parkrunning when on holiday in the UK. I was introduced by my brother who we were visiting in Shrewsbury. We looked it up here and there wasn't one in Tauranga. He said we would have to start one when we got back.

So when we got back I sent an email to Noel and Lian and I said I would be interested in setting one up and if there had been anyone else so we could get together.

I didn't hear anything for a little while and then suddenly in the local newspaper there was an article about parkrun. It transpires that Sally, our other ED, had become aware of parkrun through that and contacted Noel and Lian. This was just before Christmas. We've no idea why an article had been written!

We ended up with several others emailing and in one of those emails someone suggested the Kopurererua Valley might be a good place.

We arranged to meet there and mark it out. It seemed like a good idea, so we decided to run it on a Saturday to see what it would be like.

Then we told Noel and Lian that we had our course. Within five to six weeks we had approval. It was very quick.

My wife Jackie has never been a runner but she's now a regular. We regretted we didn't know about parkrun when we set off for Europe. We were in France and Italy and then the UK where we caught up with my brother. We could have run others! It sounds trite but I love the community feel. It doesn't matter how good or bad you think you are. I'm just your typical weekend warrior. It's good fun.

It gets you out of bed on a Saturday morning, you run, might have a coffee and you can be home fairly early and still have the whole day ahead. For some people it's given them a purpose that's reignited their lives.

We've got the best post event café surrounding in NZ because it's in the Historic Village and if you're lucky you might see a seal in the water while you're running.

 While in Tauranga...

Historic Village

Walk at Mauao (Mount Maunganui)

Mount Hot Pools

Hairy Maclary and Friends Waterfront Sculpture

McLaren Falls Park

Mount Maunganui - View from the Mount

Photo Credit - Sally MacPherson

Puarenga parkrun

Puarenga Park, Te Ngae Rd, Rotorua, 3010

Type of Course
Two laps

Shoes Required
Road or Trail

Location of start
The run starts from behind the MIGS gym car park.

Getting there by public transport
Nearest bus stop is 500m from the start, Routes 3 and 10 stop there. See the baybus website for timetable.

Getting there on foot
From the city centre follow Te Ngae Rd footpath to the Puarenga Park entrance, turn left and head towards MIGS at the rear of the car park. Alternatively follow the cycleway, accessible beside the Sudima Hotel, follow the path to the start area (do not make any turns off the path).

Getting there by road
From town/city centre and west: Follow directions for Whakatane (SH30) Te Ngae Rd, turn left at Puarenga Park (first left after the Pak n Save lights) and follow road to end.

From east: Follow signs for city centre and turn right at Puarenga Park (first right after Sala St lights).

Parking is in the tar-sealed car park (in between the buildings) or on the right beside the park. There is no time limit or charge.

 Things to know
Toilets 100m away from start, on the right as you drive through the car park. The run director opens them about 7am. Parking is free and suitable for motorhomes.

Not permanently marked

Forgotten your barcode? Email the run director the night before to print for you.

Nearest showers at Rotorua Aquatic Centre

Very low risk of cancellation (cancels annually for Rotorua Marathon, typically first Saturday in May).

 Cafe
Ciabatta Bakery on White St

 Stats

First run: June 25, 2016

Inaugural attendance: 128

Record attendance: 186 (29/02/2020)

Course Records

Women: Hannah Gapes 17:37 (17/10/2020)
Men: Paul Martelletti 15:31 (28/12/2019)

The Story Behind Puarenga parkrun

Alison King – founding co-event director

Everyone has a parkrun story and mine began a year before I ran my first parkrun.

Since 2010 I have been a regular listener of the Marathon Talk podcast, which at the time of writing was co-hosted by the Chief Operating Officer of parkrun global Tom Williams.

Over the years (I was aware of it from 2014 onwards) Tom and Martin Yelling would talk about parkrun. And it got me wondering what it was all about.

I was living in Rotorua and there was no parkrun in my small city. The nearest was a good 80 minutes drive away (Hamilton Lake parkrun) and I just didn't see any point in driving that far for a free 5km, especially when I had a two-year-old son and it was an 8am start.

My instagram feed started to show more parkrun photos, and while on the Gold Coast in 2015 for a run coaching course, I happened upon Kirra parkrun as the runners were finishing – except I hadn't looked into parkrun before I went there so missed my chance to join in.

In January 2016 I found myself in Auckland on a Friday. I was staying overnight with running friends (and they hadn't tried parkrun either). So we all registered, printed and laminated our barcodes and readied ourselves for the morning to go to Barry Curtis parkrun.

I had all kinds of ideas in my head what parkrun would be like and it was everything I expected. It was fun, low key, for everyone, and I immediately wanted the same experience for my town so I got in touch with Noel and Lian, our country managers at the time and it went from there.

The ball was rolling when I received a phone call from Jason Chapman, he'd just moved to Rotorua and had been involved with the setting up of four UK parkruns. He'd mentioned starting parkrun to another runner and learned about me. Jason's knowledge and experience has been invaluable.

There are so many places to run in Rotorua but the obvious place to run was on the sulphur flats (mostly because it met parkrun criteria).

We finally started in June 2016 and since then have welcomed parkrunners from all over the world, but mostly all over our city.

It's a very unassuming course when you arrive, it looks a bit derelict but it's when you start running that the beauty unfolds – from the manuka grove through to the moonscape.

The name Puarenga comes from the stream that we run beside (you can run beside it in the forest too). Puarenga means floating blossom and refers to the yellow sulphur deposits that float and swirl as they come down the stream.

Our parkrun might be a bit smelly and a bit steamy but it's out of this world – and the only geothermal parkrun in the world.

I love the community that parkrun has created and extending the manaakitanga (hospitality) that Rotorua is known for, to runners and walkers.

 While in Rotorua...

Redwoods Treewalk

Te Puia and Maori Arts & Crafts Institute

Skyline Rotorua

Tikitapu (Blue Lake)

Polynesian Spa

Redwoods Treewalk

Taupo parkrun

Two Mile Bay Reserve, Mapou Rd (off Lake Terrace), Taupo, 3330

Type of Course
Out and back

Shoes Required
Road

Location of start
The event starts beside the path in Two Mile Bay Reserve.

Getting there by public transport
There is no public transport available for this parkrun.

Getting there on foot
From town centre head south along Lake Terrace for 3.5 kms, 2 Mile Bay Reserve is on the lake at Mapou Rd.

Getting there by road
From town centre head south along Lake Terrace for 3.5 kms, 2 Mile Bay Reserve is on the lake at Mapou Rd.

Things to know

Toilets, drinking fountain and car parking at Two Mile Bay Reserve. Parking is free and suitable for motorhomes.

Permanently marked

Forgotten your barcode? Email the RD Friday night to print for you.

Nearest showers are at Taupo Superloo, Story Place.

Very low risk of cancellation, annual cancellation for Across the Lake Swim (usually last Saturday in February)

Cafe

There is a coffee cart at the finish.

Stats

First run: January 21, 2017

Inaugural attendance: 128

Record attendance: 141 (04/01/2020)

Course Records

Women: Hannah Oldroyd 18:05 (27/01/2018)

Men: Alex Brackenbury 16:13 (21/11/2020)

The Story Behind Taupo parkrun...

Nick Marshall, founding event director

I lived in Brisbane, Queensland, for a few years and first heard about parkrun while there.

I participated and/or volunteered quite often at various parkruns around Brisbane and thought it was a fantastic idea.

Upon moving back to New Zealand I was stoked to see parkrun was taking off in New Zealand but gutted to see there wasn't one in Taupo!

I got in touch with the country managers for parkrun NZ (Noel and Lian) and asked if they had any plans to start a parkrun in Taupo.

Their answer was that they would love to but were looking for a local enthusiast to take the reins and get it set up. So I put up my hand and the rest is history.

I liaised with the council and got set up with local sponsors then submitted my proposed course. There were a number of requirements so I had to change the course once based on this.

We ran a trial event in early January 2017 to test everything out then officially started on 21 January 2017.

Colin Little, event director

I did my first parkrun in Lower Hutt in 2015, I was introduced to it by a run director from Hagley parkrun who was on the same training course after doing some midweek runs together.

I have always just run to keep fit, not belonging to any run clubs or anything, just for my own pure enjoyment and the occasional event.

Taupo didn't have its own parkrun back then so I had to wait nearly two years to do my next one. I started volunteering shortly after and became a run director in 2018 then event director in 2019 when the current ED left to grow his family and get back into studies.

I RD more than run so still only done 83 runs to date (96 volunteer), I will get to 100 one day. We have had our first local reach 100 just prior to the lockdown.

We have a healthy mix of ages and abilities with many walkers, and a lot of visitors being a tourist destination town, in fact we quite often have more tourists than locals.

Why should visitors run Taupo parkrun? I am biased but it is just such a beautiful parkrun course, tourists comment on just how picturesque and beautiful our course is.

 While in Taupo...

Huka Falls

Craters of the Moon

Long and short walks

Taupo Bungy – New Zealand's only cliff-top bungy

Taupo DeBretts Hot Springs

Huka Falls

Photo Credit - Megan Costello

Gisborne parkrun

Waikanae Beach Playground, Grey St, Gisborne, 4010

Type of Course
Out and back in two directions

Shoes Required
Road

Location of start
The event starts by the Waikanae Beach Playground.

Getting there by public transport
There is no public transport available for this parkrun.

Getting there on foot

From Gladstone Rd/Roebuck Rd roundabout:

Head southeast on Gladstone Rd toward Carnarvon St. Go through two roundabouts before turning right onto Reads Quay. Continue along the riverside walkway for 800m.

From Balance Street Village:

Head southwest on Balance St toward Stout St. Turn left onto Stout St, then turn right onto Fitzherbert St. Continue onto Peel St. Turn left onto Reads Quay then continue along the riverside walkway for 800m.

From Kaiti Mall:

Head northwest on State Hwy 35, toward Craig Rd. Turn left onto Reads Quay, continue along the riverside walkway for 800m.

 Getting there by road
Enter Waikanae Beach Playground, Gisborne 4010 into SATNAV or google maps.

From the Gisborne i-site:

Head south on Grey St. At the roundabout, take the 2nd exit and continue along Grey St.

From Wainui (North of Gisborne):

Head southwest on State Hwy 35 toward Oneroa Rd. Turn left to stay on State Hwy 35. At the roundabout take the 2nd exit and continue along State Hwy 35. At the second roundabout, take the 1st exit onto Grey Street.

From Hexton:

Head southeast on Back Ormond Rd toward Glenelg Rd. Continue onto Ormond Rd. Turn right onto Lytton Rd. At the roundabout, take the 1st exit onto Gladstone Rd. At the roundabout, take the 3rd exit onto Stanley Rd. At the roundabout take the 1st exit onto Childers Rd. Continue along Childers Rd to Grey St. At the roundabout take the third exit onto Grey St. Continue along Grey St.

From Makaraka (State Hwy 2):

Head northeast on Main Rd, continue onto Gladstone Rd, at the roundabout take the 3rd exit onto Stanley Rd. At the roundabout take the 1st exit onto Childers Rd. Continue along Childers Rd to Grey St. At the roundabout take the third exit onto Grey St. Continue along Grey St.

Things to know

There are toilets, outdoor showers, a playground and benches at the Waikanae Beach Playground start area. There is a grassy area where children can play at the start/finish.

Parking is free and there is space for motorhome parking.

Not permanently marked

Forgotten your barcode? The library on Bright St has a printer.

Outdoor showers at the surf club by the start/finish, otherwise head to Bright St public toilets for shower facilities.

Very low risk of cancellation

Gisborne is the most easterly parkrun in the world

Cafe

There is no post-parkrun coffee venue.

Stats

First run: May 12, 2018

Inaugural attendance: 43

Record attendance: 124 (28/12/2019)

Course Records

Women: Nicole van der Kaay 16:53 (09/01/2021)

Men: Ronan Lee 15:32 (02/01/2021)

The Story Behind Gisborne parkrun...

Megan Costello, event director

I was one of the Run Directors at Batemans Bay in New South Wales, Australia. The funny thing is I helped Batemans Bay get started but I didn't really know what I was doing. They were setting it up and I was asked to come along.

My first ever parkrun was Merimbula in New South Wales. I found it because I was googling triathlon in the area and every time I googled it kept coming up.

I registered and we showed up with a stroller each. We were late and I needed the toilet but we started.

We started way behind everyone else. We were like 'what do we do with this barcode?'.

It's a boardwalk with mangroves, quite narrow out and back. You've got to be careful with people running towards you so we never made it back there again with all the young kids, it was too difficult getting out the door for 8am.

We moved to Batemans Bay and I joined a group of women who were training for various events, like triathlons or ultras. They do the City to Surf year after year in Wonder Woman costumes.

I joined them through a friend and I did a couple of test runs [at the new parkrun]. Then I started doing more and more volunteering and the next thing you know I was an RD.

We left when the parkrun was about one and a half. Because I was a regular RD I was halfway to milestones 50 [runs] and 25 [volunteers].

I didn't want to quit there and Rotorua and Anderson were a long way to go from Gisborne.

We've lived in Gisborne previously and I had a lot of contacts. In the first week I talked to a couple of people about getting it started.

One was Quentin Harvey who works for Sport Gisborne Tairawhiti. The two of us worked to develop where the course was going to be.

Initially it was a bit confusing. I had the same name as the Event Director for Anderson!

We were a little slow off the mark. At first our course wasn't going to meet the criteria. Doing the paperwork and the risk assessment we probably could have got it going earlier than we did but life got in the way.

We were all set to go and then Tauranga and Wanaka jumped ahead of us.

A lot of people have said they can't believe Nelson doesn't have a parkrun but I had the confidence to set it up because I knew how easy it was once you got over the initial hurdles. It doesn't take up much of your time.

We met up with the Gisborne Harriers before we started. Last year they got some funding and hired someone to revamp their programme. At the local sports awards they won the club of the year and parkrun won community impact.

I think it's easy if you've been RD five times, you know it's not that scary. Batemans Bay was pretty small.

I describe parkrun as a safe to fail environment. It's safe, it's free. If you screw it up you won't have spent much money. And the people are really understanding.

We don't get many parkrunners coming because we're the most easterly, it's usually because they're coming to visit family or they're wanting to tick off another New Zealand parkrun.

We're pretty hard to get to but that being said, Grant Lincoln from Barry Curtis parkrun has come enough times that we recognise him.

The value I get from our parkrun is getting to know our community and seeing them away from parkrun.

 While in Gisborne...

Farmers market Saturdays 9.30am

Makorori Beach

Whataupoko Mountainbike Park

Climb Kaiti Hill

Eastwoodhill Arboretum, biggest arboretum in the southern hemisphere

Anderson parkrun

Anderson Park, 515 Kennedy Rd, Greenmeadows, Napier, 4112

Type of Course
Two big laps, one small lap

Shoes Required
Road

Location of start
The event starts near the skate park.

Getting there by public transport
There is no public transport available for this parkrun.

Getting there on foot
Starting at the Napier supermarkets follow Kennedy Rd towards Taradale for approximately 5.5km. Starting at McDonald's Taradale follow Gloucester St towards Napier for approximately 2km.

Getting there by road

From the north: Follow State Highway 2 to the Napier Inner City exit. Turn right onto Kennedy Rd.

From Hastings: Follow State Highway 2, using the Napier inner city exit, turning left into Kennedy Rd.

From the city centre: Follow Kennedy Rd to Anderson Park.

The car park at the corner Auckland Rd/Kennedy Rd is the closest car park to the finish line.

Things to know

A toilet block is close to the car park at corner Auckland Rd and Kennedy Rd, a children's playground and skate park is in the same vicinity. Two further car parks are along Kennedy Rd and some roadside parking is available too. There is also a barbecue area.

Parking is free and there is space for motorhome parking.

Permanently marked

Forgotten your barcode? ? Email the event team and they may be able to print a spare for you.

There are no nearby showers but contact the event team ahead of your visit to make arrangements

Very low risk of cancellation

Cafe

Cafe Florian, in Greenmeadows New World supermarket

Stats

First run: May 28, 2016

Inaugural attendance: 97

Record attendance: 161 (15/02/2020)

Course Records

Women: Hannah Oldroyd 17:57 (24/02/2018)
Men: Chris Sanson 15:26 (05/01/2019)

The story behind Anderson parkrun...

Louise Shambrook, member of the founding team

My husband Philip sold the concept of parkrun to me.

He was in Bendigo studying for his Ph.D and parkrun launched there around the same time he arrived - July 2015.

He came home in the December and organised a meeting at Bay Espresso, Karamu Rd, inviting about 10 people who he thought might be interested in starting a parkrun in Hawkes Bay.

We'd first become aware of parkrun at a Regional Sports Organisers' conference in Hawke's Bay in 2013. We were busy running the Hawke's Bay Trail Series and the Kaweka Mountain Marathon that we had recently developed and launched.

At that meeting Nneka Okonta had mentioned that she was looking to start a parkrun in Hawke's Bay and was looking for support. We didn't have any free time then but thought it would be a great opportunity to provide a good community event.

Roll on to late 2015 and this first meeting. There were 10 people there and they included existing parkrunners from England and Wellington, who now lived in the Bay, plus runners from various groups we knew, a gym owner keen to promote fitness and people Philip thought might have an interest in the project.

Everyone was enthusiastic about starting parkrun and so Philip returned to his Ph.D studies in Australia, leaving the group to run with the project.

Between us we put together the official parkrun paperwork, talked to the council for permission to use the chosen park and committed to volunteering in the first six weeks. Early discussions resulted in deciding to try to hold the parkrun nearer Napier, thinking there was a large target population, including it being a popular tourist centre. It was a knock-out process to choose the location and after several rounds of voting Anderson Park was the winner.

Then started the negotiations and discussions with Napier City Council. It was a painful process, with little progress for weeks. It seemed that the junior or middle managers either could not grasp the parkrun concept, or were just unsupportive.

Weeks passed and numerous meetings. It was looking unlikely that we were going to get council agreement. It was all very frustrating.

At long last we got to talk with a more senior manager at the council - they seemed to immediately "get it", saying a group of volunteers want to hold weekly, free events, for the benefit of the community at no cost to and with no input from council - why wouldn't we approve it - or words to that effect.

So Anderson parkrun launched 28 May 2016 - effectively almost six months later. Anderson parkrun now has a strong, enthusiastic contingent of parkrunners every week.

My first parkrun was in March 2016 at Bendigo, when I visited Philip over there.

So, despite being one of the founders of both Anderson and Flaxmere parkruns, my debut was over in Australia about three months before Anderson was launched.

 While in Napier...

Art Deco Tours

National Aquarium of New Zealand

Ōtātara Pā Historic Reserve

Self-guided tour of the Sea Walls

Te Mata Peak

Photo Credit - Flaxmere parkrun

Flaxmere parkrun

Flaxmere Park, Swansea Road, Flaxmere, 4120

Type of Course
Three laps

Shoes Required
Road

Location of start
The event starts just opposite the Swansea Rd car park. If you park in Henderson Rd, walk into the park and then walk anti-clockwise until you reach the start.

Getting there by public transport
There is no public transport available for this parkrun.

Getting there on foot
The start is across the road from the Flaxmere shops within walking distance for most Flaxmere residents.

Getting there by road
From Napier/Hastings Expressway (SH50A) leave expressway at roundabout with Flaxmere Ave and York Rd. Follow Flaxmere Ave. Turn left onto Henderson Rd, left onto Swansea Rd, car park is on the left opposite the shops.

Additionally, roadside car parking is possible along Henderson Rd or Flaxmere Ave, which would necessitate a short walk to the start.

Things to know
Toilet block near start/finish. Children's playground near start/finish. Parking is free and there is street parking for motorhome parking.

Permanently marked

Forgotten your barcode? Email the event team and they may be able to print a spare for you.

There are no showers nearby.

Very low risk of cancellation

Cafe
There is a coffee cart on-site

Stats

First run: June 15, 2019

Inaugural attendance: 144

Record attendance: 144 (15/06/2019)

Course Records

Women: Eva Goodisson 18:25 (10/08/2019)

Men: Antony Jackson 16:50 (25/12/2020)

The story behind Flaxmere parkrun...

Philip Shambrook, founding event director

I had been parkrunning in Australia for a few years before returning in October 2018.

I was planning to set up another parkrun in Hawke's Bay so it was simply a matter of finding a team of people and a location.

The team was easy. The issue was finding somewhere suitable.

We wanted a nice location with access to toilet facilities and coffee. While we have kilometres of flat, limestone trails for cycling, running, and walking we did not like any of them for a new parkrun.

We had almost given up when someone mentioned Flaxmere Park.

Flaxmere is a suburb of Hastings that you tend not to go to unless you live there or have a reason but it turned out to have a park that might have been made for parkrun.

On our first visit we walked one lap of the park and

found it measured 1.7km. The path around the park is winding, shaded from established trees and with a great sealed surface. It was ideal. From then on it was plain sailing.

We decided right from the beginning that we needed to work with the community so we set up a first meeting with the council and the local community leaders.

That was probably the best thing we did as the Flaxmere demographic is largely Pacific Islanders and Māori and quite insular.

Council and the community were then on board from the beginning and worked with us to deliver Flaxmere parkrun within four months from first meeting to first event.

We could have probably launched earlier but ended up arranging the launch to tie-in with Matariki, opening of a new children's playground and the launch of a housing initiative.

If there is anything to highlight about the setting up of Flaxmere parkrun it would be the need to be aware of the community. I was instrumental in getting Anderson parkrun going in as much I brought together the event team while I was home from Australia in December 2015.

In that case there were no community members involved, just council.

While it might be that Napier Council and Hastings District Council are different, it is clear that Napier Council is not as involved or interested in Anderson parkrun as Hastings Council is with Flaxmere parkrun.

Why should people visit Flaxmere parkrun? It's a nice flat course on winding sealed paths. During the summer large established trees provide shade virtually all the way around the course.

The park is one of the unsung gems in Hawke's Bay and well worth a visit in its own right. It has also been awarded the title of New Zealand's Most Active Park.

Flaxmere Park is a pretty park all year round. However, in spring the fresh green growth of the trees and the grass imbibe the park with vibrancy and life.

In summer, the grass can get brown and look tired but the green trees provide welcome shade. And in autumn the colors as the leaves change provide bursts of colour that are in stark contrast to the greens of the grass.

 While in Flaxmere...

Pekapeka Wetlands

Splash Planet

Wineries and Cellar Doors

Gannet Safari at Cape Kidnappers

Hawkes Bay Farmer's Market every Sunday

East End parkrun

Nobs Line, Strandon, New Plymouth, 4312

Type of Course
Out and back

Shoes Required
Road

Location of start
The event starts on the grassy area, between Fitzroy and East End Surf Clubs.

Getting there by public transport
There is no public transport available for this parkrun.

Getting there on foot
Along the walkway from town: Follow walkway along the beach until you see East End Surf Club on your right. Start line will be on the grassy area between East End and Fitzroy Surf Clubs.

Along the walkway from Bell Block: Follow walkway along the beach until you see Fitzroy Surf Club. Start line will be on the grassy area, between Fitzroy and East End Surf Clubs.

Getting there by road

From town: Continue along Devon St and turn left into Nobs Line. Veer left and head towards the car park near East End Surf Club.

From Bell Block: Turn right at the traffic lights after the Waiwhakaiho Bridge onto Devon St East. Turn right into Nobs Line and head towards the car park near East End Surf Club.

Parking spaces can be found around East End Surf Club as well as Fitzroy Surf Club. There are also parking spaces past the surf club around the East End skate park and indoor hockey rink as well as neighbouring streets.

Additionally, roadside car parking is possible along Henderson Rd or Flaxmere Ave, which would necessitate a short walk to the start.

Things to know

Toilets, beach access, children's playground if you follow Nobs Line down past the skating rink and across the bridge.

Free parking with parking suitable for motorhomes.

Not permanently marked

Forgotten your barcode? Email the event team and they may be able to print a spare for you.

Cold showers (people quite often will jump in the sea)

Very low risk of cancellation

Cafe

The Kiosk at the Fitzroy Surf Club

Stats

First run: September 22, 2018

Inaugural attendance: 109

Record attendance: 138 (21/09/2019)

 Course Records

Women: Hannah O'Connor 17:48 (25/05/2019)

Men: Nathan Coombes 16:21 (06/07/2019)

The Story Behind East End parkrun...

Trevor Masters, founding event director

It probably started with (co-ED) Erin. In the end I had a discussion with her at another event. I was thinking about setting it up and she had already made contact so we joined forces.

I was in Sydney in March 2012 and a friend of mine told me about it. I went to St Peters [the first in Sydney] and thought it was fantastic. I thought it would go well here but it was still early days.

I didn't get much support for it because it was still very new to New Zealand so I put it on the back burner.

I always thought the obvious place for a parkrun in

New Plymouth was Pukekura Park but council weren't keen on that at all. The second choice was by one of the streams in town but parkrun didn't like that. They felt a couple of bridges were too narrow.

The final run was chosen almost spontaneously and it's been great. We take it for granted – it's a run I do quite regularly anyway. I'd run a couple of parkruns before we started but I'd never volunteered before.

I don't think we had any expectations. We were overwhelmed with numbers and a bit of pressure on the timing, making sure everyone was okay. We'd not run a test event so it was a bit terrifying! But it was great.

We didn't know what we were growing but looking at it now it's incredible to see the number of families who come along. It's very rewarding. I was doing it for my own selfish reasons, which is ironic because I hardly get to run any more.

 While in New Plymouth...

Pekapeka Wetlands

Coastal Walkway

Brooklands Zoo

Pukekura Park

Len Lye Centre

Goblin Forest

Pukekura Park

Whanganui Riverbank parkrun

Whanganui Riverbank, Opposite 282 Taupo Quay, Whanganui, 4501

Type of Course
Out and back in two directions

Shoes Required
Road

Location of start
The event starts on the Whanganui Riverbank opposite 282 Taupo Quay.

Getting there by public transport
There is no public transport available for this parkrun.

Getting there on foot
Walk (or cycle) 2 kilometres downstream (south-west) along the riverbank from the i-SITE, 31 Taupo Quay.

Getting there by road

Follow Taupo Quay from the i-SITE, 31 Taupo Quay.
The starting area is a grass area beside the Mountains
to Sea Cycleway opposite 282 Taupo Quay.

Parking is available along both sides of Taupo Quay.
Please use the official railway crossing into the park.
Bikes can be left in the park.

Things to know

24 hour toilets are 2km away at 75 St Hill St.

Parking is free and there is space for motorhome parking.

Not permanently marked

Forgotten your barcode? The library on Pukenamu Drive
is open until 6pm.

Nearest showers are at Splash Centre, London St.

Very low risk of cancellation (annual cancellations for
Three Bridges Marathon and Cemetery Circuit,
motorcycle race both held in December).

Cafe

Columbus Coffee (Mitre 10 Mega)

Stats

First run: July 4, 2020
Inaugural attendance: 76
Record attendance: 83 (11/07/2020)

Course Records

Women: Mackenzie Morgan 18:48 (01/08/2020)
Men: George Lambert 15:55 (01/08/2020)

The Story Behind Whanganui Riverbank parkrun...

Judy Mellsop, event director

Walking round Western Springs park in Auckland catching glimpses of my younger son running was my first experience of parkrun.

Soon after we were visiting Rotorua so I joined him at Puarenga parkrun to walk my first event and before I knew it was doing a parkrun any weekend we were out of town getting ideas for establishing an event here.

I'm very unsporty and have never been involved with competitive team sport but have walked for exercise, sightseeing and to get around most of my life.

I could see parkrun would be a great way to get locals with a wide range of ages and abilities out exercising in my community without necessarily being competitive.

So, without too much thought and with no idea of the hiccups and hurdles I'd encounter I clicked the 'start a new parkrun' button on the parkrun website.

After many setbacks our launch date was set a year after that initial inquiry. Then New Zealand went into

135

lockdown, delaying our inaugural event by another three months.

As hard as I tried I couldn't get my first two route choices to work due to road crossings and the need for a straightforward course.

We finally settled on a course along the banks of New Zealand's longest navigable river. Legal personhood was granted to the river in 2017. It has special cultural importance to the Māori people and was a major transport route for early Europeans.

The river's mood is constantly changing due to lifting fog, the rising sun and tides. Birds and river craft including waka ama (outrigger canoes) come and go.

I'm particularly looking forward to seeing newcomers begin exercising.

It's good to get out and exercise, with parkrun you don't have to be competitive so it suits a wide range of people.

 While in Whanganui...

Durie Hill War Memorial Tower

Virginia Lake

Bushy Park Wildlife Sanctuary

Whanganui River Traders Market

New Zealand Glassworks

Whanganui River

Photo Credit - Richard Berber

Palmerston North parkrun

Manawatu Riverside walkway, Victoria Esplanade,
Palmerston North, 4410

Type of Course
Out and back

Shoes Required
Road

Location of start
The run starts on the footpath near the Fitzherbert Bridge
on Fitzherbert Ave, Hokowhitu, Palmerston North.

Getting there by public transport
Number 12 or 14 bus from the Main Street Terminal, last
stop before crossing the bridge.

Getting there on foot
From Hardie St Reserve/Centennial Dr carpark: Head
towards the river walkway, the start line is right near the
Fitzherbert Bridge.

From Victoria Esplanade carpark: Follow the path towards
the river walkway.

Getting there by road
Head south on Fitzherbert Ave towards the bridge and either turn right into Victoria Esplanade gardens or turn left to park at Hardie St Reserve or along Centennial Dr.

Things to know
Toilets, drinking fountain within 50m of start/finish line. Parking is free and there is space for motorhome parking.

Not permanently marked

Forgotten your barcode? Head to the Central Library in The Square to print out.

Nearest showers at Palmerston North City i-Site.

Very low risk of cancellation (flooding risk but not affected parkrun yet)

Cafe
The Elm Café, 283 Fitzherbert Ave

Stats
First run: October 28, 2017

Inaugural attendance: 217

Record attendance: 278 (01/02/2020)

Course Records

Women: Phoebe McKnight 16:56 (13/01/2018)

Men: Luke Scott 14:37 (05/12/2020)

North Island

The Story Behind Palmerston North parkrun...

Kate Southern, founding event director

It was born out of "Why don't we have one here?" after I saw people sharing it on social media.

I'd not run one before but I saw that the parkrun community was quite a strong community in terms of support, encouragement and people getting in behind each other, especially for the beginner runner who had always thought about wanting to build up to a 5km.

I saw that and I wanted to be part of it. Initially it was for selfish reasons.

I wasn't planning to set it up but it turns out just about anyone can do it with the right frame of mind behind you.

It came to be that I'd contacted parkrun NZ at the same time that another woman had contacted them. We got put in touch with each other and formed a small committee.

We got it off the ground within six months from the initial contact and our inaugural event was in October 2017.

It probably began like a lot of others, we thought our river path would be a perfect spot for a parkrun.

We're the same as other parkruns I'm sure in that we've had people who come along to walk and then they start to jog some and then run the whole way. Then they start entering things like 10km events.

It's a good, safe place for people to begin that journey. There's excitement about having people around you, too.

I think our course is quite a fast one. We've held the New Zealand parkrun record. It's a good one to PB on as it's fast, flat and asphalt all the way.

The river is beautiful any time of the year, I think as locals we take it for granted but when you put on tourist eyes it's really pretty.

 While in Palmerston North...

Heaps of other walking tracks, including the Manawatu Gorge

National Rugby Museum

Te Apiti Windfarm lookout

Palmerston North Esplanade Scenic Train

Arapuke Mountain Bike Trails

He Ara Kotahi bridge

Manawatu Gorge

Photo Credit - Andy Walmsley

Greytown Woodside Trail parkrun

Greytown Woodside Trail, near Woodside Station 5794

Type of Course
Out and back

Shoes Required
Road

Location of start
The event starts on the Greytown Woodside Trail. From the car park, turn right and walk 100m to the start of the trail. You will see a sign above an archway that says Greytown Woodside Trail. The start is 100m down the trail.

Getting there by public transport
There is no public transport available for this parkrun.

Getting there on foot
From Greytown follow the Rail Trail route from the Cotter St start point.

Getting there by road
From State Highway 2, turn on to Humphries St (next to Challenge petrol station at intersection), then continue on, eventually leaving Greytown. Humphries St becomes Woodside Rd, which leads to Woodside Station. Please do not turn on to Cotter St. The parkrun starts at the Woodside end of the trail. It is about 5km from Greytown. You will see the station just beyond the railroad tracks.

Things to know
Parking is at the Woodside Railway Station, space for motorhomes to park. Toilets at the railway station.

Permanently marked

Forgotten your barcode? Email the event team and they may be able to print a spare for you.

No nearby showers

Very low risk of cancellation

Cafe
The Offering, 65 Main St, Greytown

Stats

First run: November 3, 2018
Inaugural attendance: 42
Record attendance: 81 (18/01/2020)

Course Records

Women: Hannah Oldroyd 18:19 (08/12/2018)
Men: Matthew Moloney 16:23 (09/02/2019)

The Story Behind Greytown Woodside Trail parkrun...

Dave White, event director

I ran the first parkrun at Lower Hutt in May, 2012. I was curious about it. I ran down that trail all the time. I read about it in the local newspaper and thought I'd go along and see what it was about.

I liked that it was free, measured and timed. You just show up and they do all the work. It was fun, I enjoyed it.

You hang around afterwards and talked to other people. Then Lucy and I moved to the Wairarapa. I wondered why we didn't have one.

Phil and I met while running. I started a local running group here called South Wairarapa Runners. Bruce McCardle was also a member of that group – he was also one of the Lower Hutt originals.

We started talking about parkrun and we scoped out different ideas for a course. Lucy suggested the rail trail, we checked it out and Phil was a trustee.

We would not have the parkrun community that we have without The Offering.

147

Phil Cox, event director

My first parkrun was here. It hadn't really taken off in the UK when I left in 2009. When we ran and Dave talked about parkrun it piqued my interest.

I'd wanted the rail trail to be used more. It's been a great community drive. The hotels and pubs are talking about parkrun. People are coming to Greytown to do parkrun.

 While in Greytown...

Visit Schoc Chocolate

Kahikatea Gardens

Cobblestones Museum

Go shopping – discover the owner-operated shops with a walk along the streets after your cafe experience.

Explore Greytown one tree at a time. From the enormous Australian Eucalypt outside St Luke's Church on Main St to the beautiful Soldiers Memorial Park Plantings and 1921 Lime Trees on Kuratawhiti St.

Spot the Tui in the trees

Kapiti Coast parkrun

Otaihanga Domain, Makora Rd, Otaihanga, Paraparaumu 5036

Type of Course
Out and back

Shoes Required
Road

Location of start
The runs starts in Otaihanga Domain, Paraparaumu. Take the path towards Waikanae River. Cross swing-bridge then walk upstream to the parkrun start.

Getting there by public transport
Take the train to Paraparaumu Railway station, then Bus 262 Paraparaumu – Paraparaumu Beach (via Mazengarb Rd). Get off at Manly St.

Walk to Otaihanga Park via Kotuku Dr, Petrel Cl, foot-track, Makora Rd. (Total walk 2km)

From Waikanae Railway Station – Bus 280 Waikanae Station – Waikanae Beach – Waikanae Station. Get off at Barret Dr. Walk south along Queens Rd until you get to Weggery Dr.

Walk along Weggery Dr until you get to the path to the Waikanae River. Cross the swing–bridge and head up stream to the start area. (Total walk 1.4k).

Getting there on foot
See public transport directions.

Getting there by road
From the north: Follow State Highway 1 to the Peka Peka/Waikanae exit. Keep right to continue onto Hadfield Link Rd, follow the road to the left. Continue onto State Highway. At the roundabout take the second exit onto Otaihanga Rd. Follow Otaihanga Rd and continue onto Makora Rd.

From the south: Follow State Highway 1 to Kapiti Rd, turn right, then turn left onto Arawhata Rd and continue onto Mazengarb Rd. Turn right onto Ratanui Rd, turn left onto Otaihanga Rd and continue onto Makora Rd.

Look for parkrun flags at the entrance to the domain.

From the Waikanae side: Park car on Weggery Dr. Take path towards Waikanae River. Cross swing-bridge then walk upstream to the parkrun start.

Things to know
The domain has two toilet blocks, ample parking and a playground for the kids. Park in Otaihanga Domain. Parking suitable for motorhomes

Permanently marked

Forgotten your barcode? Head to the Warehouse Stationery for printing.

Nearest showers at Coastlands Aquatic Centre

Very low risk of cancellation

Look out for cockatoos in summer

Cafe
There is a coffee cart on-site

Stats

First run: January 24, 2015
Inaugural attendance: 205
Record attendance: 205 (24/01/2015)

Course Records

Women: Hannah Oldroyd 18:19 (17/02/2018)
Men: Paul Martelletti 15:30 (01/01/2020)

The Story Behind Kapiti Coast parkrun...

Jude Wadsworth, stalwart volunteer

Andy Jenkins, my son-in-law, was going to Porirua parkrun, which is about a half hour drive away and he thought it would be nice to not have to get up quite so early.

There were Kapiti people going to Porirua so he thought he could start on here.

He went to council and had one route down the side of the stream but council said they would be closing that path – we'd already had a test run.

It was closing for the expressway so we worked with Kapiti Coast Council to find somewhere else.

They put in permanent markers for us and have been a really good supporter of parkrun.

At the inaugural run I was on finish tokens and that's evolved to doing the volunteer roster and whatever job needs to be filled.

Andy has been event director for five years. I've only ever done a couple of freedom walks – I prefer to be there to support Andy; I'm so proud of what he's done.

It's an amazing event. Apart from Andy, my biggest reason for supporting it is to have a family event where families can come and all have they have to pay for is to get there and back.

Our numbers go up and down because of winter sports. We don't see every family week after week but when it's between seasons we see them. I love it. It's a real family event.

I knew a lot of people already but it's definitely extended my community.

I'm usually on finish tokens but scanning is good, especially with the new technology and you get to know people that way.

One thing about our parkrun is the birdlife – in summer we have Australian cockatoos on the course.

Paekakariki Escarpment Track

While in Kapiti...

Kapiti Island

Southward Car Museum

Paekakariki Escarpment Track

Ngā Manu Nature Reserve

Kapiti Chocolate Factory

Photo Credit - Julie Swiden

Porirua parkrun

Bothamley Park, 77 Champion St, Cannons Creek, Porirua 5024

Type of Course
Out and back

Shoes Required
Road

Location of start
The run starts at the corner of Windley and Champion
Streets, Porirua.

Getting there by public transport
Bus route 226, stop number 2302. Please check timetable
before leaving home.

Catch the train to Porirua railway station on the Waikanae
line and walk 1.5km via Mepham Pl and Champion St to
the start.

Getting there on foot
Bothamley Park has many entrances and is friendly for
walkers. Just follow the stream to the parkrun start.

Getting there by road

From State Highway 1 turn off at the Mungavin Interchange and head to Porirua East on Mungavin Ave. At the Z Petrol Station turn left into Champion St. Follow Champion St until the Windley St intersection.

Park on Champion St inside the white line and walk the short distance from Champion St to Bothamley Park (signposted).

 Things to know

Ample free parking with parking suitable for motorhomes.

Permanently marked

Forgotten your barcode? Email the RD to print for you or print at the library

Nearest showers at Terauparaha Arena

Very low risk of cancellation

 Cafe

Porirua McCafe, McDonalds on Lyttelton Ave

 Stats

First run: July 6, 2013

Inaugural attendance: 71

Record attendance: 275 (01/01/2020)

 Course Records

Women: Hannah Oldroyd 18:09 (27/05/2017)

Men: Paul Martelletti 15:47 (09/05/2015)

The Story Behind Porirua parkrun...

Astrid Van Meeuwen-Dijkgraaf, founding event director

My husband was over in the UK and discovered parkrun but he didn't run one.

He came back and said he needed to get fit and wondered if we had one here. That's how we discovered Lower Hutt parkrun. He went along and then I started to join him.

It was a bit silly driving half an hour to do a half hour parkrun. We thought we should set one up of our own.

We spent three months looking for somewhere in Porirua to have a parkrun. We tried out all kinds of routes but none worked for us. I mentioned it to someone at council and they suggested Bothamley Park and that was how we got started.

We hadn't run that many before we thought about it, it was maybe three or four months. Thirty minutes isn't that far but we thought if we could set up our own we could sleep in a bit, but that didn't work out as we ended up getting up even earlier.

We were event directors for almost six years and then I decided I needed a break. We were really fortunate because we went to talk to the council about using the track in their park and they were at the point wanting to improve the park and had a five year budget.

It wasn't somewhere you would go unless in a group. They cleared lots of vegetation. We came along and said Lower Hutt gets 60-80 and we could manage 60 most weeks.

They were very supportive and advertised on the council website. They had a fortnightly council newspaper and advertised it there a couple of times.

Word got around fairly quickly.

There were a number of people who were living in or close by going to Porirua parkrun who had been going to Lower Hutt.

It's always been enthusiastically received and grew gradually. We've put up a humongous billboard on State Highway 1. Council asked us what we wanted and they delivered. We've had huge support from them. They've been really awesome.

Some of the council staff have even become RDs. We've been very lucky.

It's a lovely walk or run through the forest beside a stream. We're really friendly. Most people who have been say it's the nicest parkrun they've been to.

It's in a gully so even if it's howling it's not that windy. On windy days we get quite a lot of Lower Hutt people turning up.

Our sign has been photographed a lot.

Because the start line is away from the road it's reassuring to new people that they're in the right spot.

One person came along and was into bird photography, we've bird hides along the Pautahanui Inlet.

What I really enjoy about parkrun is the community it's built. We really noticed it during the lockdown, People you never would have met previously running virtually together still.

For us, one of the reasons we set up parkrun was we had already lived here five years. It's a small street but we didn't feel like there was much of a community.

So for us parkrun has allowed us to connect to our community and that's really important. That's also why we stepped back. We didn't want it to be ours, we wanted it to be our community's.

While in Porirua...

Titahi Bay beach

Mana Island

Zealandia

Plimmerton Beach

Camborne Walkway

North Island

Photo Credit - Gina Foster

Trentham Memorial parkrun

Trentham Memorial Park, Brentwood St, Trentham, Upper Hutt, 5018

Type of Course
Riverside out and back

Shoes Required
Road

Location of start
Start is 95m along the path from the Holdsworth Ave entrance to Trentham Memorial Park, or 250m from the Brentwood St car park.

Getting there by public transport
Trentham train station is located in Ararino St, Trentham. The Hutt Valley Line operates between Wellington and Upper Hutt and the current timetables are available on Metlink website. The Wairarapa train line operates between Masterton and Wellington, but only stops at Upper Hutt train station. There is a bus stop at the carpark entrance 43 Brentwood Street, Metlink bus route 114 operates between Upper Hutt and Trentham train stations. Please see metlink.org.nz for current timetables.

Getting there on foot
From the Trentham train station in Ararino St, head down Totara St to Fergusson Dr. Trentham Memorial Park is on the other side of the road. Cross the road when safe.

Follow the path through the park, past the playground on your left and car park to the right, towards the start/finish line.

Getting there by road
From the South: Exit State Highway 2 at the Silverstream Bridge exit, travel along Fergusson Dr for 3.8km and turn left into Brentwood St. Car park entrance is at 43 Brentwood St.

From the North: Exit State Highway 2 at the Moonshine Rd exit and take your first right into Holdsworth Ave. Turn left into Brentwood St and proceed to the car park entrance to Trentham Memorial Park.

The start is 250m from the car park.

Things to know
Toilets are near the Brentwood St entrance. There is a children's playground nearby.

Free parking available in Brentwood St car park.

Forgot your barcode? Email the RD to print for you.

Nearest showers are at the H20 Xtream Aquatic Centre, corner of Brown and Blenheim Streets.

Very low risk of cancellation

Not permanently marked

Cafe
Fig Tree Café, 386 Fergusson Dr, Heretaunga, Upper Hutt

Stats

First run: January 30, 2021
Inaugural attendance: 257
Record attendance: 257 (30/01/2021)

 Course Records

Women: Saskia Knox 19:08 (30/01/2021)
Men: Thomas Strawbridge 17:11 (30/01/2021)

The Story Behind Trentham Memorial Hutt parkrun...

Allan Hartley, event director

Astrid from Porirua parkrun organised a pop-up in December 2019, it was rained out, which was good as I couldn't go. Originally it was Astrid's idea and she had no idea I lived here.

I've been here the last five years and had often thought about a parkrun here because it would be just that little bit closer to home.

I don't think she had any intention of operating it, she just wanted to plant the seed, she was successful.

We sat down with the council in January and started progressing things, then Covid hit. By then we had the course done, council approval – they've been really

165

supportive from the start – and just needed the funding.

I first heard about parkrun from the local newspaper back in 2012. My running buddy was injured and I'd found it hard to keep myself motivated to run.

Lower Hutt parkrun was launching the next week so I went along. I thought it was brilliant so I kept on going. At the time I had a New Zealand Home Loans franchise and they ended up sponsoring parkrun.

I liked the fact there was a whole bunch of other people; that I wasn't doing it alone.

When it came along I thought it was motivating. Looking back it changed my whole weekend.

I'd beaver away all week with work, then get to Saturday and blob out and do not a lot. But when you had to get up and go for a run at 8, it turned into 'what can I do next'. My wife noticed a change to our whole weekend, I'd get more done.

 While in Upper Hutt…

Remutaka Rail Trail

Kaitoke Regional Park

Aston Norwood Gardens

Visit Kereru Brewing Company

Expressions Whirinaki Arts & Entertainment Centre

Trentham Memorial Park - Photo Credit - Stu Leslie

Photo Credit - Lower Hutt parkrun

Lower Hutt parkrun

Riverside Parking, Daly St, Lower Hutt, 5010

Type of Course
Riverside out and back

Shoes Required
Road

Location of start
Start is just south of the southern end of Riverside Parking, accessed from the roundabout on the junction of Daly St and Andrews Ave in Lower Hutt. The local landmark is the City Fitness Gym which is immediately over the stopbank and across the road from the start/finish area.

Getting there by public transport
By train from Wellington or Upper Hutt, take the train to arrive at the Waterloo Interchange, no later than 7.15am.

Then catch the number 160 Wainuomata to Lower Hutt bus from bus stop D to the Queensgate bus stop C in Bunny St. From there, walk west along Bunny St (south side of the Westfield shopping centre) and along Margaret St to High St. Turn left and walk down High St to Andrews Ave and then right into Andrews Ave.

At the end of Andrews Ave walk up on to the stopbank and south 200m to the start/finish area.

The Melling train line from Wellington does not run on a Saturday.

Getting there on foot
See above.

Getting there by road
From Wellington or Upper Hutt, travel along State Highway 2 until you reach Melling.

Drive over the Melling Bridge and turn right at the roundabout onto Melling Link. Turn right onto Rutherford St, turn right into Daly St just after King Toyota. Follow Daly St south until the next roundabout and then turn right up the short hill over the stopbank and into Riverside Parking. Park at the south end of the car park.

Do not access the car park at the first roundabout in Rutherford St as this will take you to the Riverside Farmers Market.

Things to know
Toilets are 300m from the start in Riddiford Gardens. Free parking is available in Riverside Parking, limited to two hours.

Not permanently marked (there are km markers but start, finish and turnaround not obvious)

Forgotten your barcode? Print out at one of the libraries (Te Awe Library is nearest to city centre), or Warehouse Stationery.

No showers nearby

Very low risk of cancellation

Cafe
Buzz Café, 101 High St, Lower Hutt

Stats

First run: May 5, 2012

Inaugural attendance: 84

Record attendance: 327 (11/01/2020)

Course Records

Women: Phoebe McKnight 16:59 (13/01/2018)

Men: Edwin Kaitany and Nick Horspool 15:25 (05/05/2012 and 01/01/2015)

The Story Behind Lower Hutt parkrun...

Richard McChesney, original event director

When I arrived back in New Zealand from the UK in 2012 I contacted Noel and Lian about starting a parkrun up in Lower Hutt. I saw them in mid February and more or less started working on getting it started straight away.

It had to be beside the Hutt River I thought so I started looking at different options in the Hutt area.

Initially it was going to start on the other side of the river because there was a car park by the church and I arranged with the church to use the car park.

But two or three weeks before we were due to start we had a whole lot of rain and there were too many puddles. We would have gone up the trail on the opposite side of the river to Melling, then down the stopbank to the Ava railbridge, over the bridge and along the stopbank to finish where we now start and finish.

It's a slightly different course to what it is now. We changed it because it would have otherwise discouraged people in winter, so we decided to go out and back at the last minute.

We almost had an unknown runner as our first finisher at our first event. Edwin Kaitany is a Kenyan runner, he was in New Zealand training with Wellington Scottish for a short period. When he finished he had left his barcode in his car and said not to worry about getting his result recorded. He ended up going back for it. Nine years later and he still has the course record!

In Week 7, Paul Sinton-Hewitt came to visit. We had hail during our parkrun and 38 finishers. I think that is the only time we have had hail during Lower Hutt parkrun. When I said I wanted to start parkrun in New Zealand Paul thought it was a good chance to catch up with Noel and Lian.

On the Friday night we had a drinks night at the local pub so a few (maybe 10-15) parkrunners came along, not that parkrun meant a huge amount to them, because we were still only seven weeks old. Now, if Paul was to visit again, I'd imagine that the pub would be full of parkrunners.

We were about 20 weeks old when I found out I was going to be in Dublin for six weeks. We had a core team and Kent Stead had already started helping at that stage. At the time he was event director for Swimming NZ, he became a run director while I was in Dublin and Mark Malone got involved too. They then got other volunteers so we had lots of the roles filled rather than just a few of us doing everything.

Going away was good because it forced us to get a good crew together in a short time. Kent and Mark managed to organise a lot of that. I moved back to the UK at the end of April in 2014 – it was the week before Lower Hutt's birthday so we brought our annual celebration forward!

Seven years later, and Lower Hutt is still recorded as my home parkrun – and always will be.

 While in Lower Hutt...

Walk Te Whiti Riser for harbour views

Visit Kaitoke Regional Park

Walk to Pencarrow Lighthouse

Petone Settlers Museum

Matiu/Somes Island

South
Island

Photo Credit - Alison King

Blenheim parkrun

Corner of High and Symons Streets, Blenheim 7201.

Type of Course
Out and Back

Shoes Required
Road

Location of start
The run starts from the edge of the boardwalk at the Amphitheatre on the Taylor River.

Getting there by public transport
There is no public transport available for this parkrun.

Getting there on foot
Walk to the Amphitheatre in town and go down to the boardwalk by the Taylor River.

Getting there by road
From the north: Follow State Highway 1 into Blenheim. Turn right onto Main St, then right onto Symons St, follow the road around and park in the Farmers' car park.

From the south: Follow State Highway 1 into Blenheim. At the roundabout keep on Main St and turn right onto Symons St, follow the road around and park in the Farmers' car park.

Things to know

Toilet and free parking (until 9.30am) at the Farmers car park. There is space for motorhome parking.

Not permanently marked

Forgot your barcode? Email the RD to print out, printing also at Warehouse Stationery

Nearest showers at Stadium 2000.

Very low risk of cancellation

Cafe

Thomas & Sons, 54 Market St, Blenheim.

Stats

First run: July 9, 2016

Inaugural attendance: 27

Record attendance: 85 (28/12/2019)

Course Records

Women: Hannah Oldroyd 17:36 (20/10/2018)

Men: Gus Marfell 15:59 (02/01/2021)

The Story Behind Blenheim parkrun...

Phil Muir, event director

I owned the Blenheim New Zealand Home Loans branch and up until 2019 they were the national sponsor.

I do a bit of running but more multisport and mountain biking. I wanted to get parkrun up and running but I knew that I couldn't do it on my own. That's where Oliver (Carne) came in. He was from the UK and trying to get a police job in New Zealand.

He popped into the office one day and asked if we'd heard of parkrun and if we would be interested in starting one up.

That's where it all kicked off in terms of knowing there were people other than myself who were interested.

We'd asked a shop earlier – they were doing a Tuesday run – then we let it sit for 12 months.

In the end we were like, "well this is what we're doing, are you able to promote it?"

Part of the reason I got involved was the NZHL sponsorship, but like any other parkrun it's down to the local people to get it going. It's not necessarily all

179

the big centres, it's where people are who have had affiliation with parkrun before.

We usually get small fields, in winter around 25-30 runners. One thing that surprised me was the level of international interest.

Marlborough is quite common visitor destination and we get a lot of people coming along on a Friday night to do parkrun.

Some people come over from holidaying in Nelson since they don't have a parkrun. We have an office in Nelson and we've looked for a course there but we've not found anything suitable yet.

I've found two things about parkrun after starting it up. One is the tourism and having people from overseas, they stay on the Friday so they can do parkrun.

The second is hearing stories from people who just want to do something as group but at their own pace. It eases themselves back into movement, whether it's after having kids or an operation, or those who just want to lose a bit of weight.

 While in Blenheim...

Omaka Aviation Heritage Centre

Take a wine tour

Walk the Queen Charlotte Track

Short walks in Picton

Take a cruise in the Marlborough Sounds

The Queen Charlotte Track

Pegasus parkrun

Lake Pegasus, Pegasus Town, North Canterbury, 7612

Type of Course
Two laps in summer, out and back in winter.

Shoes Required
Road

Location of start
The start is on the grass area near the stairs leading to the lake.

Getting there by public transport
The 95 leaves Christchurch for Pegasus Town. Go to metroinfo.co.nz for the timetable.

Getting there on foot
Pegasus parkrun is easily accessed from the town centre by heading towards the lake.

Getting there by road
From State Highway 1 take the Pegasus Town exit onto Pegasus Blvd. Follow the road, continuing through the roundabouts, until you reach Pegasus Main St. Turn left onto Pegasus Main St and follow the road to Lakeside Rd. Car parking is on either of these streets.

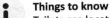

Things to know

Toilets are located on the grass area near the corner of Pegasus Main St and Lakeside Dr. Car parking can be found along Pegasus Main St, Lakeside Dr and on the road approaching the suspension bridge

Parking is suitable for motorhomes

Permanently marked

Forgot your barcode? Print at Warehouse Stationery in Rangiora.

There are no showers nearby

Very low risk of cancellation

Pegasus operates a summer and winter course

Cafe

The Flat White, on the corner of Pegasus Main St and Pegasus Blvd.

Stats

First run: June 18, 2016

Inaugural attendance: 61

Record attendance: 247 (21/04/2018)

Course Records

Women: Hannah Oldroyd 16:53 (09/06/2018)

Men: Matthew Dryden and Nick Burrow 15:49 (23/09/2017 and 22/12/2018)

The Story Behind Pegasus parkrun...

Geoff McMillan, founding event director

I discovered parkrun, after I had a life-altering event. I had a sudden cardiac arrest on June 26, 2011.

After going through the recommended therapy clinics I began to get involved in duathlon events, however my run sections were dismal to say the least.

I struggled along for a couple of years and one day toward the end of 2014 decided that if I could find some 5km events (a fairly common distance in duathlon) that would help.

Google's first response was to bring up Hagley parkrun – a weekly 5km run in Christchurch and best of all, it was FREE! I followed the prompts, registered and my first ever parkrun (which was only the 10th for Hagley) was underway.

I was hooked. I work from Christchurch five days a week and after a number of Hagley parkrun events I began to think along the lines of where in North Canterbury could this concept take shape?

I talked with some people in the running community about possible sites and the potential for the idea.

In the end I had three sites to decide between and just the one authority to gain agreement from. The course around Lake Pegasus fitted the bill perfectly.

It had hosted both triathlon and duathlon events in the past, there was a "natural" 2.5km circuit, so two laps meant spectators and volunteers could see and encourage people midway and at the finish.

It was all looking pretty good, but then my Mum's health began to fail and I shelved the idea in order to better help her.

After her passing I needed to refocus and one of the first things I needed to do was get this new parkrun event up and running, so I got in touch with Lian and Noel de Charmoy.

We met, went over the course and within a couple of weeks Pegasus parkrun was underway. It was a great feeling to see 62 parkrunners at our inaugural (it was very close to a 50/50 split in regard to locals and tourists).

Late 2019 I surrendered my role as event director at Pegasus to become the first South Island event ambassador, so while Pegasus remains my home parkrun, I now consider myself to be of a wider group of parkruns.

 **While in Pegasus...**

Visit the Te Kōhanga Wetlands

Visit Woodend Beach & Tuhaitara Coast Park

Play a round of golf at the acclaimed Pegasus Golf Club

Go winetasting in the Waipara Valley

Wander around the heritage buildings of Rangiora

Photo Credit - Alex Slack

Hagley parkrun

North Hagley Park, Rolleston Ave, Christchurch 8013.

Type of Course
A figure of eight, single lap

Shoes Required
Road

Location of start
The run starts at Victoria Lake next to the Botanic Gardens Armagh St car park in North Hagley Park.

Getting there by public transport
Please see the metro website for details.

Getting there on foot
Hagley Park can be accessed from a number of entry points on foot.

Armagh footbridge off Rolleston Ave

Rolleston Ave

West Bridge off Riccarton Ave

Woodland Bridge off Riccarton Ave

Getting there by road
Access the Armagh St car park via Rolleston Ave and
Lake Tce.

Things to know
There are public toilets next to the Rolleston Ave car park
and over footbridge into the Botanic Gardens. Children's
playground and paddling pool over footbridge into
Botanic Gardens.

Free parking, also suitable for motorhomes

Not permanently marked

Forgotten your barcode? Email the Run Director to see if
they can print out for you.

No showers nearby

Very low risk of cancellation

Cafe
Ilex café, Botanic Gardens visitor centre

Stats

First run: October 4, 2014

Inaugural attendance: 82

Record attendance: 523 (25/01/2020)

Course Records

Women: Angie Petty 16:40 (23/12/2017)

Men: Oska Baynes 14:29 (05/12/2020)

The Story Behind Hagley parkrun...

Brad Henderson, founding event director

My wife and I lived in Melbourne from 2006 to 2014, when we moved back to New Zealand to raise a family.

I was involved in the setting up of Albert parkrun in 2011, which was the third event to start in Australia and the first out of Queensland. I wasn't part of the event team but I knew the event director and I was there on opening day. I did some run directing and ran it a lot.

We left just prior to parkrun exploding in Australia. When we left there were only a handful of events in Melbourne, now there are so many that I've lost track.

We came back here and the first thing I said was "let's go to parkrun" and there wasn't one.

I got in touch with Lian and Noel and asked if they had they heard from anyone about setting one up in Christchurch and they said there'd been a couple of inquiries. They put me in touch with Jo Taylor, she was really keen. Her brother was involved with parkrun in Australia.

She wanted to launch in April but my wife was pregnant and going into winter probably wasn't the best time. When we first planned our route my idea was to run around South Hagley Park.

I planned out a route that seemed to work quite well. Then Richard McChesney came down one weekend, he was about to head back to the UK and wanted to see our course.

It was a horrible day in the middle of winter. As I took him round he pointed out a number of driveways that would need marshals – I'd never thought of that. He asked if we had any other options – we did, North Hagley Park.

One of the other guys in our crew had made a course that had no crossings and was totally contained, it was a no brainer so we shifted to that one.

It's not a pure figure of eight but close enough. It's pretty unusual; there are lots of single loops, double lappers or out and backs at other parkruns.

We had 82 at our first event and it gradually grew in popularity. Me and Jo were run directors for most of the first year. I've since stepped aside as event director but I'm still a run director. Every year it gets bigger, which is great to see. We have the highest attendance in New Zealand (523) which we're pretty proud of.

I've made some great friends through it.

Based on people I've talked to it's more than a run, they come for the social connection than the run itself.I come from a running background so parkrun isn't about fitness. I train hard at other times.

It's about connecting with people. It's got something for everyone and that's the beauty of it, whether you're a 16 minute runner or doing the run/walk thing. That's what we love about it, the diversity of speeds, gender and ethnicity.

Hagley Park

While in Christchurch...

Explore Hagley Park and the Botanic Gardens

Quake City Museum and Air Force Museum

New Brighton Pier

Visit Quail Island

International Antarctica Centre

Foster parkrun

Foster Park, Broadlands Drive, Rolleston, 7614

Type of Course
Out and back with a loop in the middle

Shoes Required
Road

Location of start
The event starts near the hockey turf close to the main car park.

Getting there by public transport
From the Christchurch Central Bus Exchange take the Yellow Line bus to Rolleston. Buses to Rolleston are also available from Lincoln and Burnham.

Getting there on foot
Carpark A is opposite the Aquatic Centre and next to the playground. The start and finish is by the Hockey Turf, a one minute walk south of the car park.

Getting there by road

From Christchurch follow State Highway 1 south to Rolleston, turn left after the BP onto Tennyson St. Follow Tennyson St straight through the two roundabouts until it becomes Springston Rolleston Rd. At Rolleston College turn right at the roundabout onto Broadlands Rd. Foster Park is on the left opposite the Selwyn Aquatic Centre.

Car parking is available beyond the playground, carpark A, Broadlands Dr (opposite Aquatic Centre).

Things to know

Public toilets, picnic tables, car parking, and "one of the coolest playgrounds in the country". Parking suitable for motorhomes.

Not permanently marked

Forgotten your barcode? Email the RD to print one out

Nearest showers at Selwyn Aquatic Centre over the road

Low risk of cancellation

Visit in spring for daffodils and wild flowers

Cafe

Robert Harris Café, 76 Rolleston Drive, Rolleston

Stats

First run: October 27, 2018

Inaugural attendance: 205

Record attendance: 205 (27/10/2018)

Course Records

Women: Hannah Oldroyd 17:48 (10/11/2018)

Men: Dan Bennetts 16:48 (13/04/2019)

196

The Story Behind Foster parkrun...

Suzy and Greg Petersen, event directors

Suzy: We started going to Hagley on their fifth event. We lived in town at the time so it was pretty easy to get to. Then we had Ali and pretty soon after she was born I told Greg that our house was too small.

We bought out at Lincoln and it was a half hour trip to Hagley. It started to get old. As part of the core team parkrun was what we did. We started scouting out places that would be good for a parkrun and then we found Rolleston, it's the biggest town in Selwyn and most central. We figured we would get people from West Melton, Lincoln, Rolleston itself and southern suburbs of Christchurch.

It took us a year as when we started talking to the council Foster Park was still in the process of being developed. It had previously been farmland.

They were making rugby, football and hockey pitches and a T-ball diamond. It took a year to finish the paths.

Greg: It was a very long year. We had put out feelers to say we were going to start a new parkrun and we had a good initial reaction and people came forward but then we had this hiatus of waiting for footpaths to be finished and for grass to grow.

Even since we've started some of the park works have been ongoing – they're building a $25 million indoor sports centre at the moment.

Suzy: The week of our inaugural we found out Josie was on her way and it was a busy time, but it was great. Our girls are growing up knowing this is what we do on a Saturday unless there's sickness.

Greg: There's no getting out of it when you've got all the gear! We've been really amazed with how the community has taken to it. One of the things that I've been mindful about is the founding principles of parkrun. When I do something I go into it like down a rabbithole. I bought the book *parkrun: much more than just a run in the park*. I really started looking at the philosophy and principles behind it.

Neither of us are athletes. We're in it for the greater good.

Suzy: I'm in it for the coffee!

Greg: We're all about encouraging everyone to come, even if it's people who maybe a bit lonely in the community. People with mental health issues. We've not put up any barriers and are welcoming to everyone to the point where we're quite protective of our parkrunners. parkrun is for everyone and you're only running against yourself. It's getting people into society and talking.

Suzy: We made some really good friends at Hagley and Foster. You might not see them during the week but you're pretty happy when you see them on the weekend. There are three main families with young kids. All the volunteers are happy for the kids to hang around if they don't want to finish and we all keep an eye on them. We'll quite often still be there at the hour mark.

Greg: It's seeing people in our community participate, getting out and being active on a Saturday morning.

When it came to courses, Porirua struck me as an out and back, having that interaction with the faster runners.That's an element we tried to include. The way we've got it is there's no bottlenecks.

While in Rolleston...

Explore the Selwyn District's bike trails

Wander around Rolleston's gardens

The Canterbury Astronomical Society in West Melton holds public open nights most Fridays

Go ballooning over the Canterbury Plains

Lincoln Farmers Market is on every Saturday from 10am to 1pm

Queenstown parkrun

Queenstown Beachfront and Gardens, Marine Parade,
Queenstown 9300

Type of Course
Two laps

Shoes Required
Road

Location of start
The event starts at the Queenstown beachfront,
Marine Parade.

Getting there by public transport
Queenstown ORBUS Blue Peaks bus stop is closest. Start
line is approximately 500m from bus stop.

Getting there on foot
From town, walk to Queenstown beachfront near the
corner of Earl Street and Marine Parade. The event start/
finish is on the beachfront footpath leading into
Queenstown Gardens near the public toilets.

Getting there by road
From Queenstown airport, take Frankton Rd-6A towards
Queenstown town centre. Continue on Frankton Rd into
Queenstown Gardens. Alternatively, continue on 6A into
Queenstown town centre and take a left on Ballarat St.
Take a left on Camp St and follow around until Marine
Pde.

Parking can be found for free in and around
Queenstown. Paid parking can be found in Queenstown
town centre.

Closest to the parkrun start are paid car parks lots,
which are on Church St and Ballarat St. Parking is
suitable for motorhomes.

 Things to know
Toilets 20m from the start and water fountains on the
course. There is both free and paid car parking in and
around the town centre.

Not permanently marked

Forgotten your barcode? Ask your hotel to print for you,
or head to Warehouse Stationery in Frankton

Nearest showers at Alpine Aqualand

Very low risk of cancellation (cancelled annually for
Queenstown Marathon in November)

**Note: 9am start in New Zealand Standard Time (winter),
8am in New Zealand Daylight Saving Time.**

 Cafe
Yonder Café, 14 Church St

Stats

First run: June 9, 2018
Inaugural attendance: 93
Record attendance: 172 (23/11/2019)

 Course Records

Women: Caitlin Adams 17:41 (06/10/2018)
Men: Paul Martelletti 15:32 (04/01/2020)

The Story Behind Queenstown parkrun...

Chris Seymour, founding event director

I started running parkrun in Sydney. Before moving to New Zealand, I lived in Australia for eight years.

I'd gotten into distance running and one of my colleagues was a triathlete. He said I should check out parkrun and told me how to find my closest event.

After looking it up and thinking it was pretty cool, I joined in at St Peters parkrun in 2016 which was the first in Sydney. I loved it.

Two years later my wife and I decided to move to Queenstown full time for a lifestyle change – we had some land and had built a holiday house.

We started looking up the closest parkruns and there

was none. I heard that Wanaka was going to start one and that town was smaller than Queenstown and still 100km away.

I thought to myself "how could Queenstown be the tourism capital of the South Island and not have a parkrun?".

One reason I wanted to get to a parkrun was I didn't know anyone and thought the running community was where I would meet like-minded people.

I reached out to Noel and Lian from parkrun NZ through the normal channels and they told me they were coming to Wanaka and I should meet up with them.

Chatting with a couple of runners in a local run group, I asked about parkrun interest and they said it would be cool to have in town.

I ended up mapping out a course myself with a couple of different options.

After Wanaka's inaugural event before Noel and Lian were going to depart from Queenstown I offered to take them on the course. My wife and Lian had coffee at a potential parkrun café while I took Noel around Queenstown Gardens.

He said he thought it would be the most beautiful course in all of New Zealand.

"I think you will get most parkrun tourists of any

parkrun in New Zealand," he said. Every week (pre covid) about 40-50% of our runners are from somewhere else.

The interesting thing with Queenstown is it's a transient population. People come in and work seasons. They'll work a ski season or be a summer rafting guide.

We have a core group of locals but then there are people who are quasi-local. They live here for a season and come to work but eventually they move on.

It's interesting because Queenstown has a big trail running community. A lot of our core volunteers are ultra-marathon and mountain runner types. They'll volunteer and then as soon as we're done, they're putting on their vests and getting out their poles and heading on a mountain or trail run mission.

We also have a lot of talented kids at the local high school. The track coach is involved as a volunteer and brings his up and coming runners to test at our event.

We're also a Q, which is a hard one to get for the parkrun Alphabeteers.

We have views of the Remarkables Mountains and they're pretty and unrivalled. I'm not biased in any way but it's a beautiful view, especially in winter if you have a clear day, with the snow-capped mountains across the lake.

Our event is run through the botanical gardens then

through a pine forest, so you pop out and go from super sunny to completely shaded. When you leave the forest, you get the view of the Remarkables and Lake Wakatipu.

Every tourist goes OMG when they see the mountains, it's almost like you have to remember to turn.

You don't want to get too stunned by the view and end up in the lake!

It's a gently undulating course but you get a little bit of everything, footpaths, trail, forest, lake views, mountain views.

We're centrally located so it's easy to get to. If you stay anywhere in central Queenstown it's no more than a 10 minute walk.

 While in Queenstown...

Bungy jump where it all began

Ultimate Queenstown zipline with Ziptrek

Jet boating

Winery Tours

Cookie Time Cafe

Wanaka parkrun

Wanaka Station Park, Homestead Close, Wanaka 9305.

Type of Course
Out and back

Shoes Required
Road

Location of start
The event starts in Wanaka Station Park.

Getting there by public transport
There is no public transport available for this parkrun.

Getting there on foot
From Wanaka town centre, walk out of town towards Glendhu Bay on the lakefront path. After the wooden footbridge take the steps up to the left in to Wanaka Station Park.

Getting there by road
From Wanaka town centre, drive out of town towards Glendhu Bay on Wanaka/Mt Aspiring Rd. Turn right on to Homestead Cl. Turn right into the car park. The start line is located through the pedestrian gate. Very limited parking at the start/finish line, park nearby.

Things to know

Toilets are located in the park. There are shower and changing facilities nearby. Free parking, motorhome parking available at Homestead Close and Stoney Creek car park (not overnight).

Not permanently marked

Forgotten your barcode? Email the RD to print for you.

Showers at Ballantyne Road Service Hub

Low risk of cancellation

Note: 9am start in New Zealand Standard Time (winter), 8am in New Zealand Daylight Saving Time.

Cafe

Wineglass Café, Edgewater Resort, 54 Sargood Rd

Stats

First run: February 24, 2018

Inaugural attendance: 190

Record attendance: 134 (28/12/2019)

Course Records

Women: Olivia Burne 17:36 (14/07/2018)

Men: Janus Staufenberg 16:07 (25/08/2018)

The Story Behind Wanaka parkrun...

Adam Sharman, founding event director

My wife Jane is from Balclutha, but she used to come to Wanaka for holidays.

We met in Australia and when we moved to New Zealand we moved to Auckland and ran at Cornwall Park, this was it's 20th event back in 2012.

We had spent 18 months in Europe and had come across parkrun there but I hadn't run one.

By the time we arrived in New Zealand Lower Hutt had started, then Cornwall Park. We were four years in Auckland. (Adam has run more than 100 times at Cornwall Park). Then we moved to Wanaka and as soon as we knew we were going to move we thought about setting it up.

That was November 2016 and in February 2018 we started.

We wanted to show off the place as much as possible so we wanted to hold it on the lakefront. We looked at a few different options but we wanted to start in a park. In town it's beautiful but Wanaka Station Park is a very under-used reserve and not many people know it exists.

We thought it needed to be used more. It's also great for parking.

There's a nice natural tunnel of willow trees that changes through the seasons. From there you can go to the lakefront. We go by the famous Wanaka tree then along the lakefront.

For some reason people forget that if you run downhill you have to run back up it on the way back.

It really is beautiful, it's a good honest course as well. The hill is only for 60-70 metres but the lakefront course is all off road.

There's some undulation in there. People think it's a fast course but it's not, it's a strong course.

The beauty is amazing.

I always think of parkrun as the world's most positive cult. Everyone is always friendly, the attitude is always positive.

The community involvement as well, you get the high school cross country team doing time trials and other groups coming along. One of the GPs has started prescribing it because of the health benefit.

I love the fact that it's not competitive but only as much as you want it to be. It's very good to see your own improvement and have your own race with the people around you.

I love the ethos behind it; the average finishing times getting lower and that's a positive thing because that means participation is going up.

You can go anywhere in the world if you look hard enough you can find one and it will feel just like you're home.

We get a lot of visitors, in the summer it can be 60-70%.

 While in Wanaka...

Puzzling World

Roy's Peak Track

Walks in and around Wanaka

Wildwire Wanaka

Warbirds and Wheels

Walks in Wanaka

Photo Credit - Tania Hollis

Dunedin parkrun

Dunedin Botanic Garden, Opoho Road, North Dunedin,
Dunedin, 9016

Type of Course
Two sets of two laps

Shoes Required
Road

Location of start
The run starts in the lower garden near the Croque-
O-Dile Café.

Getting there by public transport
Bus: Orbus routes 5, 6, 8, 10, 11, 15 all stop at the Botanic
Garden. See the Otago regional council website for
details.

Getting there on foot
The starting point is in the lower garden just near the
cafe, toilets, glass house and information shop. From any
entrance of the lower garden, head straight to the
buildings in the middle.

Getting there by road

From the centre of town follow State Highway 1 northwards. Stay in the right hand lane, turning right at the stop sign onto Cumberland St. The Botanic Garden car park is on your left.

From State Highway 1 southwards, on driving into Dunedin, down the hill, the Botanic Garden car park is on your left after a left turn to Northeast Valley. Alternatively there is street parking along the Northeast Valley turn, Great King St.

Things to know

There is limited free parking in the car park, and ample free street parking along Great King St and Opoho Rd, which is also suitable for motorhome parking.

There are two public toilets in front of the New World car park as well as in the Botanic Garden below the Croque-O-Dile Café. Also in the Botanic Garden is a play area not far from the finish line and further up the hill there is aviary.

Not permanently marked

Forgotten your barcode? Email the event team and they may be able to print a spare for you.

No showers nearby

Very low risk of cancellation

Note: No dogs or buggies allowed. 9am start in New Zealand Standard Time (winter), 8am in New Zealand Daylight Saving Time.

Cafe
Croque-O-Dile Café

Stats

First run: January 11, 2014

Inaugural attendance: 68

Record attendance: 276 (01/02/2020)

Course Records

Women: Rebekah Greene 18:57 (14/07/2018)

Men: Joshua Baan 16:59 (02/05/2015)

The Story Behind Dunedin parkrun...

Emma Laurence, founding event director

The idea came from my parents, Ross and Carol Haddow. Dad was a run director at Sheringham parkrun in the UK at the time. My husband and I were into our sports, like running, triathlon etc and mum said we needed a parkrun in our area.

We didn't have one so she suggested we set it up. I thought that was crazy but then we thought we could do it. I got in touch with Noel and Lian and it took a while to get it together. The main thing was finding a good venue because Dunedin is quite hilly.

The flatter places needed more laps and there was no café. There was another out and back with no café and it was quite exposed. The parks in Dunedin aren't huge so would need to be five laps.

The Botanic Garden meant we could do two laps of the bottom and two of the top. There's toilets, a café and it's sheltered. It ticked all the boxes for us.

When we started we got about 80 at the most and it's flourished. We had no idea what it was about when we started. It was before we had children and I felt unfulfilled and like I had too much time on my hands.

I thought it would be fun. I liked the idea of a community while running, that it was free and run by volunteers.

Adrian and I were the main run directors for our first 18 months and then he got a job in Auckland so we moved up there.

We're back in Dunedin now with two children aged three and five - I certainly don't feel unfulfilled now.

I'm grateful for it keeping on so I can tap into it. It's fun to see it from the other side.

Tania Hollis, event director

About eight years ago I was doing Couch to 5k, I was living in Rockingham in Australia and looking for somewhere to do my 5km.

parkrun had just started up there, the first time I went I volunteered to see what it was all about. Then I did my first 5km.

It was such a nice community.

Then in 2015 I moved back to Dunedin. I knew for about a year that I would be coming back, there wasn't a parkrun here and I thought I'd have to start it up.

Shortly after I had that thought the parkrun started up here. I contacted the ED (Emma Lawrence) to say I would be happy to help out. She and her husband then moved up to Auckland and I joined the group who volunteered to keep it going.

I've never mentioned this before but the thing with parkrun is you don't need the confidence to be an event director.

By doing parkrun you ease into it by doing a little bit of volunteering. By the time you become ED you're very familiar with how it all works.

I feel I'm the caretaker for Dunedin parkrun, when there comes a time when I want to step back the next caretaker will step in, it's nothing to do with me personally.

Dunedin is a bit hilly. We're very lucky to be in the Botanic Garden. However Emma managed to swing that is amazing. In Dunedin there aren't many places you could do a 5km that would fit parkrun's requirements.

Doing our loop-the-loops certainly works. Because we're restricted in the garden we do two laps in the bottom section and then you head over the river into the top section, which is where the hills are and the stairs of despair. You go twice around that.

It's amazing the people who don't listen to the first timer's briefing, often they try to get out of doing the second lap on the top hilly loop!

parkrunners should come here to enjoy the Botanic Garden and do the hardest parkrun in New Zealand – and meet up with a great parkrun community down here.

 While in Dunedin...

Baldwin St, steepest street in the world

Royal Albatross Centre

St Clair beach

Toitū Otago Settlers Museum

Otago Museum

Photo Credit - Rod Deverson

Balclutha parkrun

Naish Park, Charlotte St, Balclutha, 9230

Type of Course
Out and back in two directions.

Shoes Required
Road or trail

Location of start
The event starts by the duck pond.

Getting there by public transport
There is no public transport available for this parkrun.

Getting there on foot
Walking south west from the town centre along the main street Clyde St, turn right into Argyle St and walk to the park entrance on the opposite side of Charlotte St.

Getting there by road
The entrance to Naish Park is off Charlotte St opposite the junction with Argyle St. Limited parking within Naish Park, but ample on Charlotte St and nearby side roads.

Things to know

Toilets, children's playground and aviary within the park near the start of the run. Limited parking within Naish Park, but ample on Charlotte St and nearby side roads.

Parking is free and there is space for motorhome parking.

Not permanently marked

Forgotten your barcode? Email the event team and they may be able to print a spare for you.

Nearest showers at Balclutha Centennial Pool

Very low risk of cancellation

Note: 9am start in New Zealand Standard Time (winter), 8am in New Zealand Daylight Saving Time.

Cafe

Café 55, 55 Clyde St, Balclutha.

Stats

First run: May 28, 2016

Inaugural attendance: 52

Record attendance: 128 (01/01/2020)

Course Records

Women: Hannah Oldroyd 17:54 (14/03/2020)

Men: Jonah Smith 16:50 (01/01/2019)

The Story Behind Balclutha parkrun...

Rod Deverson, founding event director

I'd run about 70 or 80 parkruns in the UK, mostly at Sheffield and Sheffield Hallam, then we moved here for the good life. We had a 5-year-old and Louise was pregnant with our second. I'm from New Zealand, Louise is from Wales and we ended up in Balclutha with no parkrun.

We would drive back and forth to Dunedin and it was getting a bit tiresome. We didn't do it that many times, maybe half a dozen. It's an hour each way and with the early start we were leaving home at 6.30am to go there for a 20 minute run around.

I joked with enough people that we should do it here and someone told me to stop talking about it and just do it. It was interesting because I'd done one volunteer spot up until that point but it's given me a perspective on those who don't volunteer – that used to be me. It was a matter of seeing if we would get away with it. I didn't know what it involved but it was pretty smooth sailing to get started. I remember a conversation about setting up the route, they weren't sure about our start. The first time I got to Naish Park I thought it was awesome. The right size of park for the town. There's car parking, it was a path designed for exercise. The

227

first time I ran to the bridge and back I thought it was awesome.

We have a turnaround cone and you run back and it seems like nothing but you get to the start line and go past all the volunteers, which is nice. It's one of the best features on the course, everyone sees everyone.Then you run down to the bridge. It's a decent bridge, about 240m and the Clutha is the biggest river by volume – it has more water than the Waikato. The bridge looks cool.

People should come and run it because it's tiny. It's intimate and everyone knows everyone who is doing it. You can come for the Bushy Park experience in 2004 before it got mad and popular!

I like to think people think it's nice to have a personal meet and welcome. Everyone who comes is really valued and catered for properly and I think that's what makes us a good parkrun. We're a small family parkrun.

On an ordinary day about a quarter of the field are women and kids under 15. We've not got a whole lot of runners in Balclutha, there's only a population of 4000. We're not a university town or a tourist town.

I like running and we've a couple of people who are really fast. One was never going to do parkrun because it's not competitive. He runs marathons really fast but parkrun has changed things for him. He just loves to come and run and switch off.

Nugget Point

 **While in Balclutha...**

Visit The Catlins

Museums – South Otago Museum and Dollyworld

Walk around Lake Tuakitoto

Visit the exotic birds aviary in Naish Park

Photo Credit - Mohammed Ahmed Al Riyami

Invercargill parkrun

Southland Cricket Association Inc, 150 Gala Street, Invercargill 9810

Type of Course
One lap

Shoes Required
Road

Location of start
The event starts a short walk from the main car park on Gala St, behind the Gala St reserve with the fountain.

Getting there by public transport
There is no public transport available for this parkrun.

Getting there on foot
The cricket club is based at 150 Gala St, access to this is through the gate behind the Gala St Reserve, on the right hand side of the fountains.

Getting there by road
If you are using SATNAV the address is 150 Gala St, Invercargill.

Long term parking is available on Gala St, and behind the Gala Street Reserve outside of the main cricket club gates to the left and the right of the Club.

Things to know
Toilets, taps, water fountain, playground. Pram and wheelchair friendly course.

Parking is free and there is designated motorhome parking.

Permanently marked

Forgotten your barcode? Head to Warehouse Stationery for printing

Nearest showers at Splash Palace

Very low risk of cancellation

Note: 9am start in New Zealand Standard Time (winter), 8am in New Zealand Daylight Saving Time.

Cafe
Cheeky Llama, 134 Gala St

Stats

First run: February 10, 2018

Inaugural attendance: 103

Record attendance: 218 (01/02/2020)

Course Records

Women: Claire Nichols 18:44 (29/12/2018)

Men: Craig Iversen 16:27 (25/12/2020)

The Story Behind Invercargill parkrun...

Liz Henry, founding event director

In 2016 I was on the Gold Coast for New Year's with my sister who lived there. She made me go to parkrun (Main Beach). I came last, well, last before the Tail Walker and when I came through there were 365 people still waiting for me to finish and clapping me through. I was a bit embarrassed but also thought it was pretty cool.

My thought was if Australia can do it then what do Kiwis do, I thought we could step it up here. I came back to New Zealand, made some enquiries and saw Dunedin was my closest one, but having done my studies there, there was no way I was running up that hill in the Botanic Garden.

Later that year I went to Adelaide for a cousin's wedding and we all did parkrun (Torrens). It was a good way for everyone to get together and do something before the wedding. Again, there was a similar vibe.

After that I got thinking about setting one up in Invercargill. It took us eight months to get a course sorted. We were just about to go live, when council decided to dig up most of the park for drainage so we

233

had to wait another seven months. When we first set up we thought 60 would be a success and that was the number we gave council to get permission to run.

Six months later we were getting over 100 and they were blown away – they hadn't seen that many people in the park at that time before. About half of our field are walkers. We get feedback from visitors that we're a fast course, I think it's because we have a lot of marshals so it always seems like there's lots of people around and the time passes quicker.

We were a sought after parkrun for a while, being the world's most southerly. We might not be the most southerly any more but we're the most accessible, southerly parkrun – Invercargill is easier and cheaper to get to than the Falkland Islands.

Our course isn't a straight line and it takes you right through the park. We got third place in the 2019 International Large Urban Parks Awards. Our course gives you a good view of the park, including the rose garden collection, which was started in the 1900s.

There are still lots of reasons to come to Invercargill.

 While in Invercargill...

Transport World

Motorcycle Mecca

Tuataras in Southland Museum

Go to Bluff to the sign post

Close to walks at Te Anau and the Catlins

McLean Falls, The Catlins

Acknowledgments

So many people made this happen and have supported me throughout my parkrun life.

Noel and Lian de Charmoy and Richad McChesney, for bringing parkrun to New Zealand and indulging me with your stories.

All the event directors and run directors who spoke with me about their parkruns. Not only did they share their parkrun story but they answered all my other questions and then checked that what I'd written was accurate. They also gave permission to access photos. Thank you for all the work you have done and continue to do to ensure we all have a free 5km each week.

A huge thank you to Andy Walmsley, parkrun NZ photography ambassador, run director and all round top bloke. I've told him he should create a coffee table book of his own.

Colin Little at Taupo parkrun for recommending Alex Slack as a designer.

Alex for making my words look even better. As soon as I learned you were a parkrunner I knew this would be a great partnership.

My family for enduring this passion for parkrun even though you are not runners yourselves and wonder how I can get so enthused by a free event. Thank you for coming on some of my trips so we can explore places together.

My mum, Hilary Fraser, for taking the leap and becoming a parkrunner, so proud of your 100 runs so far and all the touring you get up to with Harriet Saker and Steve Devaney. Wish I could tour with you but the UK is a bit far!

The Stratford upon Avon parkrun team for putting up with me all those months I was in the UK and continuing to be part of my life. Natalie Jackson you inspired my Copenhagen trip.

Jason Chapman, co-event director at Puarenga parkrun. Without you and the other run directors I wouldn't have done as much touring, thank you for the joy and enthusiasm you bring each week.

Lastly, thanks to each and every parkrunner who shows up each Saturday with their barcode.

A huge thank you to everyone who volunteers at parkruns around New Zealand.

Photos taken from the various parkrun facebook pages.

Thanks for reading.

To get your free copy of

Five Ways To Make parkrun More Fun

go to the link below.

https://tinyurl.com/rwabguide